USDA

United States
Department of
Agriculture

Forest Service

**Northern
Research Station**

General Technical
Report NRS-P-114

Proceedings
23rd U.S. Department of Agriculture
Interagency Research Forum on
Invasive Species 2012

23RD USDA
INTERAGENCY
Research Forum
on INVASIVE
SPECIES
January 10-13, 2012
Annapolis, MD

This publication reports research involving pesticides. It does not contain recommendations for their use, nor does it imply that the uses discussed here have been registered. All uses of pesticides must be registered by appropriate State and/or Federal, agencies before they can be recommended.

CAUTION: Pesticides can be injurious to humans, domestic animals, desirable plants, and fi sh or other wildlife—if they are not handled or applied properly. Use all pesticides selectively and carefully. Follow recommended practices for the disposal of surplus pesticides and pesticide containers.

Cover graphic by Vincent D'Amico, U.S. Forest Service, Northern Research Station.

Manuscript received for publication August 2012

Published by:

U.S. FOREST SERVICE
11 CAMPUS BLVD SUITE 200
NEWTOWN SQUARE PA 19073

May 2013

For additional copies:

U.S. Forest Service
Publications Distribution
359 Main Road
Delaware, OH 43015-8640
Fax: 740-368-0152
Email: nrspubs@fs.fed.us

Visit our homepage at: http://www.nrs.fs.fed.us/

Proceedings
23rd U.S. Department of Agriculture
Interagency Research Forum on
Invasive Species 2012

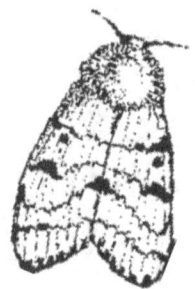

January 10-13, 2012
Loews Annapolis Hotel
Annapolis, Maryland

Edited by
Katherine McManus
Kurt W. Gottschalk

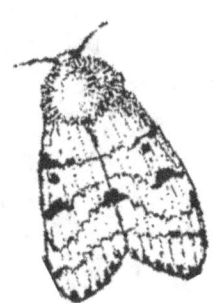

Sponsored by:

U.S. Forest Service
Research & Development

Agricultural Research Service

Animal and Plant Health Inspection Service

National Institute for Food and Agriculture

U.S. Department of Agriculture

FOREWORD

This meeting was the 23rd in a series of annual USDA Interagency Research Forums that are sponsored by the Forest Service, Animal and Plant Health Inspection Service, National Institute of Food and Agriculture, and Agriculture Research Service. The group's original goal of fostering communication and providing a forum for the overview of ongoing research among the agencies and their cooperators is being realized and facilitated through this meeting.

This meeting proceedings documents the efforts of many individuals: those who organized and sponsored the meeting, those who provided oral and poster presentations, and those who compiled and edited the contributions. The proceedings illustrates the depth and breadth of studies being supported by the agencies and their many cooperators and demonstrates the benefits and accomplishments that can result through the spirit of collaboration.

Acknowledgments

The program committee would like to thank the four USDA agencies for their continued dedication in planning the Forum, The Nature Conservancy for assistance with the registration process, and the management and staff of the Loews Annapolis Hotel for their continued support of this meeting.

Program Committee

Michael McManus, Joseph Elkinton, David Lance, Victor Mastro, Therese Poland, Michael Smith

Local Arrangements

Katherine McManus, Kurt Gottschalk

Proceedings Publication

Katherine McManus, Kurt Gottschalk

CONTENTS

POSTER PRESENTATION ABSTRACTS

THE WAY FORWARD: GUIDE TO IMPLEMENTATION OF PHYTOSANITARY STANDARDS IN FORESTRY

Gillian Allard[1] and Food and Agricultural Organization Forestry Guide Core Group and Partners

[1]Food and Agricultural Organization of the United Nations, Viale delle Terme di Caracllia, Rome, Italy

ABSTRACT

Pests and their associated damage threaten the ability of forests to provide economic, environmental, and social benefits. Expanded international trade coupled with local climatic change may increase the potential for movement of pests and their establishment in new areas. The Food and Agricultural Organization (FAO) and its partners, in collaboration with the International Plant Protection Convention (IPPC), have developed a tool to help foresters deal with these increasing threats.

The "Guide to Implementation of Phytosanitary Standards in Forestry" provides clear and concise guidance on forest health practices that will help to minimize pest presence and spread while allowing safe trade. In helping to protect forests, the guide will also contribute to efforts to reduce carbon emissions from deforestation and forest degradation (REDD).

To make the key messages of the guide even more accessible, a refresher course for forest sector personnel has been prepared as an interactive e-learning course based on the third chapter of the guide, "Good Practices for Forest Health Protection." The e-course, which has been field tested and piloted in more than 50 countries, has six modules and features a self assessment quiz at the end of each module and is available at www.fao.org/forestry/foresthealthguide/76169.

As part of the implementation phase, there has been a targeted communication effort through posters, brochures, and presentations at international fora and workshops which has contributed to an increased understanding of the role of foresters in implementation of phytosanitary standards. However, some countries still have challenges with the definition of roles and the contributions that the forest sector can make to help implement phytosanitary standards. Communication still needs to be improved, and more multi-sectoral workshops similar to that presented in Estonia in 2011 should be held.

The Estonia workshop was jointly organized by FAO and the European and Mediterranean Plant Protection Organization (EPPO) for National Plant Protection Organizations (NPPOs) and forestry sector personnel in Russian. More than 40 representatives from 15 Commonwealth of Independent States and Eastern European countries met in June 2011. This workshop brought together for the first time representatives from both the forestry and plant protection sectors, resulting in enhanced understanding and a willingness to continue dialogue and closer cooperation. A similar workshop is planned for the Balkan states for the last half of 2012, and others should follow.

AN OVERVIEW OF THE LATEST RESEARCH ON MECHANISMS OF ASH RESISTANCE TO THE EMERALD ASH BORER IN OHIO

Pierluigi Bonello[1], Don F. Cipollini[2], Daniel A. Herms[3], and Omprakash Mittapalli[3]

[1]The Ohio State University, Department of Plant Pathology, Columbus, OH 43210
[2]Wright State University, Department of Biological Sciences, Dayton, OH 45435
[3]The Ohio State University, Department of Entomology, Ohio Agricultural Research and Development Center, Wooster, OH 44691

ABSTRACT

We provided an update on the most recent research activity in the Ohio project on mechanisms of ash resistance to the emerald ash borer (EAB), *Agrilus planipennis* Fairmaire. We are using an interspecific comparative approach to determine which factors (e.g., genes, allelochemicals) render Manchurian ash (*Fraxinus mandshurica* Ruprecht), a host species coevolved with EAB, resistant to this invasive wood boring Buprestid.

Phylogenetic analysis has shown that North American (NA) black ash (*F. nigra* Marsh.), a highly susceptible species, belongs in the same clade as Manchurian ash (section Fraxinus), making this comparison presumably the most phylogenetically relevant for discovering resistance factors. However, comparisons with other susceptible and ecologically and economically important ash species, such as green (*F. pennsylvanica* Marsh.) and white (*F. americana* L.) ash, are also key to our investigations. Our results have shown that noninduced (i.e., pre-attack/constitutive) phloem of Manchurian ash differs from that of black, green, and white ash in several putative resistance factors including several genes that code for proteins known to be defensive in other systems (Bai et al. 2011, Whitehill et al. 2011) and several phenolics (Cipollini et al. 2011, Whitehill et al. 2012). We have also shown that well-known defense hormone pathways, particularly those involving jasmonates, are likely involved in the expression of resistance to EAB since topical application of methyl jasmonate protected trees in a common garden experiment to the same degree as a topical insecticide. This induced resistance was expressed in susceptible species at the same level as naturally resistant Manchurian ash (Whitehill 2011).

Most recently we have initiated experiments in which we are exploiting induction of susceptibility, brought about by techniques such as trunk girdling, in resistant species such as Manchurian ash, to dissect mechanisms of resistance even further. We are beginning to explore induced defense responses to actual EAB attack in early stages of penetration under a variety of environmental conditions, such as drought, that are highly relevant to the expression of resistance/susceptibility.

We hope to translate all this information into operational resistance programs aimed at selecting or breeding susceptible North American ash species into resistant varieties. In this context, the recent identification of potentially resistant NA ash trees (a.k.a. "lingering ash") in otherwise decimated forests (Knight et al. 2010) provides further impetus for our research.

Literature Cited

Bai, X.D.; Rivera-Vega, L.; Mamidala, P.; Bonello, P.; Herms, D.A.; Mittapalli, O. 2011. **Transcriptomic signatures of ash (*Fraxinus* spp.) phloem.** Plos One. 6: e16368.

Cipollini, D.F.; Wang, Q.; Whitehill, J.G.A.; Powell, J.R.; Bonello, P.; Herms, D.A. 2011. **Distinguishing defensive characteristics in the phloem of ash species resistant and susceptible to emerald ash borer.** Journal of Chemical Ecology. 37: 450-459.

Knight, K.K.; Herms, D.A.; Cardina, J.; Long, R.; Rebbeck, J.; Gandhi, K.J.K.; Smith, A.; Klooster, W.S.; Herms, C.P. 2010. **Emerald ash borer aftermath forests: the dynamics of ash mortality and the responses of other plant species.** In: Michler, C.H.; Ginzel, M.D., eds. Proceedings of Symposium on Ash in North America. Gen. Tech. Rep. NRS-P-72. Newtown Square, PA: U.S. Department of Agriculture, Forest Service, Northern Research Station. 64 p.

Whitehill, J.G.A. 2011. **Investigations into mechanisms of ash resistance to the emerald ash borer.** Columbus, OH: The Ohio State University. 250 p. Ph.D. dissertation.

Whitehill, J.G.A.; Opiyo, S.O.; Koch, J.; Herms, D.A.; Cipollini, D.F.; Bonello, P. 2012. **Interspecific comparison of constitutive ash phloem phenolic chemistry reveals compounds unique to Manchurian ash, a species resistant to emerald ash borer.** Journal of Chemical Ecology. 38: 499-511.

Whitehill, J.G.A.; Popova-Butler, S.; Green-Church, K.B.; Koch, J.L.; Herms D.A.; Bonello P. 2011. **Interspecific proteomic comparisons reveal ash phloem genes potentially involved in constitutive resistance to the emerald ash borer.** PLoS ONE. 6: e24863.

CHALLENGES ASSOCIATED WITH THE SPREAD OF *PHYTOPHTHORA RAMORUM* IN WATER FROM NURSERIES

Gary A. Chastagner

Washington State University, Research and Extension Center, Puyallup, WA 98371

ABSTRACT

Phytophthora ramorum, the exotic water mold that causes sudden oak death and ramorum shoot blight, has spread from nurseries into stream water in seven states. For example, in Washington, this pathogen was first detected on ornamental nursery stock in 2003. Since then, all three lineages (NA1, NA2, and EU1) have been detected in a total of 48 nurseries in western Washington. The swimming zoospores of water molds are commonly spread via water. In 2006, stream baiting revealed that *P. ramorum* had spread from a nursery in Pierce County into a nearby stream. Subsequent, yearly stream baiting has resulted in the detection of *P. ramorum* in a total of 11 drainage ditches and/or streams in five western Washington counties. Genotype analysis indicates that all three lineages of this pathogen have spread into waterways and that contamination of waterways has typically resulted from spread of inoculum from nearby positive nurseries. Stream baiting has also shown that once a waterway becomes infested, it remains infested even after successful mitigation steps have eliminated the pathogen from infested nurseries.

In the spring of 2009, infested ditch water resulted in the infection of salal plants (*Gaultheria shallon* Pursh) along the perimeter of a nursery, representing the first time the NA2 lineage had been detected on plants outside of a nursery. In 2010, additional plants tested positive in the nursery, and ditch water continued to be positive along the perimeter of the nursery. Composite soil samples collected from along the ditch were also positive in 2010, making this the first location in Washington with evidence that inoculum had spread in water from a nursery resulting in the contamination of soil and infection of natural vegetation.

The spread of *P. ramorum* in water from nurseries is a national problem that increases the risk that this pathogen and its nursery genotypes (NA2 and EU1) will spread to the landscape. The spread of the NA2 lineage to salal plants and soil in Washington illustrates the importance of this pathway. In some areas, water from infested streams is being used to irrigate a variety of horticultural sites. This also increases the risk that *P. ramorum* will spread onto plants in the landscape. There are a number of challenges associated with efforts to reduce the risk associated with the water pathway of spread. These include the complexity of riparian systems and epidemiological unknowns associated with the biology of pathogens in streams, important hosts in riparian systems, and inoculum thresholds necessary for spread via irrigation water. Regulatory challenges include issues relating to: the regulation of the disease vs. the pathogen; communicating with entities that have water rights for irrigation that water sources have been contaminated with inoculum; the failure of growers to change practices; a clear understanding of roles and responsibilities among state and federal agencies; and response to wildland detections.

Management of *P. ramorum* in waterways starts at the nursery. Other than treatment of irrigation water, there are limited ecologically acceptable mitigation options to reduce inoculum levels once *P. ramorum* spreads into a stream. Best management education and/or nursery certification programs that change grower practices relating to water management and the spread of this pathogen are needed. There is also a need to increase sampling of nursery water, particularly once the pathogen is initially detected in a nursery. Currently there are very few options for treating water leaving the nursery. Water treatment regulations focus mostly on nutrients and vary from state-to-state. The environmental acceptability of treating water with algaecides or other chemicals is unclear. Research is needed to develop low cost biofiltration systems that are effective in removing inoculum of this pathogen from water before it leaves the nursery.

Acknowledgments

The assistance of Washington State University's Katie Coats, Marianne Elliott, Kathy Riley, Annie DeBauw, and Gil Dermott, the Washington State Department of Agriculture (WSDA), the Washington Department of Natural Resources, and U.S. Department of Agriculture Animal and Plant Health Inspection Service (USDA-APHIS) is gratefully acknowledged. Portions of the work in Washington have been supported financially by the WSDA Nursery Research Program and USDA APHIS.

EVALUATING SOUTHERN APPALACHIAN FOREST DYNAMICS WITHOUT EASTERN HEMLOCK: CONSEQUENCES OF HERBIVORY BY THE HEMLOCK WOOLLY ADELGID

Yu Zeng[1], Andrew Birt[1], Maria Tchakerian[1], Robert Coulson[1], Szu-Hung Chen[1], Charles Lafon[2], David Cairns[2], John Waldron[3], Weimin Xi[4], and Douglas Streett[5]

[1]Texas A&M University, Department of Entomology, Knowledge Engineering Laboratory, College Station, TX 77843
[2]Texas A&M University, Department of Geography, College Station, TX 77843
[3]University of West Florida, Department of Environmental Studies, Pensacola, FL 32514
[4]University of Wisconsin, Department of Forest and Wildlife Ecology, Madison, WI 53706
[5]U.S. Forest Service, Southern Research Station, Pineville, LA 71303

ABSTRACT

The basic question addressed in this paper was "How will the composition and structure of southern Appalachian forest landscapes change following large-scale hemlock (*Tsuga Canadensis* [L.] Carr.) mortality caused by the hemlock wooly adelgid (HWA), *Adelges tsuga* (Annand)?" The research was conducted on Grandfather Ranger District, Pisgah National Forest, North Carolina. A spatially explicit forest landscape model, LANDIS-II (referred to hereafter as LANDIS), was used to simulate forest dynamics of the Grandfather Ranger District. LANDIS was parameterized and calibrated for 36 tree species growing in 11 distinct ecological zones. Placement of the 36 species was based on information from published literature and data from a comprehensive field survey. Vegetation dynamics were simulated under two contrasting scenarios: (1) with hemlock trees (i.e., forest dynamics before HWA invasion); and (2) without hemlock trees (i.e., forest dynamics following large scale HWA mortality). The output of each simulation was a temporal series of species abundance maps that were analyzed to understand the long-term effects of hemlock mortality on southern Appalachian vegetation dynamics. We found that species abundance increased by amounts ranging from 25 to 74 percent in landscapes without hemlock compared to those with hemlock. The number of species with abundance greater than 50 percent increased from 2-4 to 5-7 in most ecological zones. Simulations without hemlock also resulted in greater amplitudes in species abundance over time, indicating a more unstable pattern of successional dynamics. Our results suggest that the predicted, large-scale removal of hemlock from the southern Appalachian forest landscape by HWA will ultimately increase the abundance of less shade-tolerant species such as pines (*Pinus*) and oaks (*Quercus*) and substantially change forest composition and structure. Additionally, the removal of hemlock may drive an extended period of unstable vegetation dynamics that can have important implications for forest management. Finally, the model system developed for this study can be extended to explore various forest restoration strategies that have been proposed to mitigate the impacts of HWA such as the introduction of HWA resistant hemlock species, the reintroduction of native hemlock, and the implementation of mountain laurel control.

COLORS, ODORS AND TRAP DESIGNS FOR ENHANCING EMERALD ASH BORER DETECTION CAPABILITIES

Damon J. Crook[1], Krista Ryall[2], Peter J. Silk[3], Joseph Francese[1], and Victor C. Mastro[1]

[1]USDA APHIS, PPQ, CPHST, Buzzards Bay, MA 02542
[2]Natural Resources Canada, Great Lakes Forestry Centre, Sault Ste. Marie, ON P6A 2E5 Canada
[3]Natural Resources Canada, Atlantic Forestry Centre, Fredericton, NB E3B 5P7 Canada

ABSTRACT

In 2011, the standard survey trap used nationwide by the U.S. Department of Agriculture, Animal and Plant Health Inspection Service, Plant Protection and Quarantine, Emerald Ash Borer Cooperative Program (USDA APHIS, PPQ, EAB) was a glued, purple prism trap, baited with two semiochemical lures of Manuka oil (50mg/d) + (3Z)-hexenol (50mg/d), hung at 6 m in the subcanopy of an ash tree. A more user-friendly non-glued trap would be desirable because tens of thousands of glued traps are currently deployed and discarded at the end of each year. Recent electroretinographic assays and trapping work have shown that light green traps catch significantly more emerald ash borer (*Agrilus planipennis* Fairmaire) adults (especially males) than traps of other colors (Crook et al 2009). Light green traps typically catch more adults only when deployed high in the tree canopy. Thus, trap placement as well as color and lure combination must be considered when evaluating traps for a monitoring program. Francese et al. (2010) recently improved the attractancy of light green (540 nm) prism traps by adjusting the reflectance of the green to 49 percent (i.e., creating a darker green). When this dark green color was incorporated into funnel traps and then field tested alongside standard purple prism traps in an unbaited study, dark green funnel traps caught significantly more beetles when hung at 5-8 m (Francese et al. 2011). Funnel trap catch was improved further by coating the trap surface with Rain-X®. In 2011 field tests, nontinted Fluon® was shown to significantly increase trap catch on green funnel traps compared to green tinted Fluon® and to Rain-X® coated traps.

Up until 2011, no lures had yet been tested on dark green funnel traps. Two types of host volatiles, bark sesquiterpenes (found in Manuka and Phoebe oil) and leaf volatiles (particularly [3Z]-hexenol), have been demonstrated to be attractive to *A. planipennis*. The first putative long-range pheromone for *A. planipennis* was identified as (3Z)-dodecen-12-olide ([3Z]-lactone) by Bartelt et al. (2007) although no behavioral activity was reported. Silk et al. (2011) demonstrated that (3Z)-lactone significantly increased male trap catch when combined with the green leaf volatile, (3Z)-hexenol, in light green prism traps deployed in the canopy. Captures of males with the (3Z)-lactone + (3Z)-hexenol were at least 50-100 percent greater compared to the (3Z)-hexenol alone. It appears that two cue modalities are required by *A. planipennis* in the host and mate-finding process: a visual cue (green) and a two-component olfactory cue (the foliage volatile or kairomone [3Z]-hexenol and the sex pheromone [3Z]-lactone). By fine-tuning each of these three components, it should be possible to improve trap effectivity even further.

The main aim of our 2011 research was to test the latest dark green funnel traps with the most promising available lures. The lure treatments were:

1. unbaited green funnel control

2. green funnel trap baited with Manuka oil (50mg/d) + (3Z)-hexenol (50mg/d)

3. green funnel trap baited with (3Z)-hexenol (50mg/d)

4. green funnel trap baited with (3Z)-hexenol (50mg/d) + (3Z)-lactone (80ug/d)

Field tests on dark green funnel traps were carried out along the edges of infested white (*Fraxinus Americana* L.) and green ash (*Fraxinus pennsylvanica* Marsh.)

wood lots in Michigan (n=15), as well as Ontario, Canada (n=17). U.S. field sites contained ash trees with moderate to severe levels of decline. Canadian field sites contained ash trees with low levels of decline. Rain-X® coated dark green funnel traps were set within 2 m of tree stands, spaced 20-30 m apart in a randomized complete block design. Traps were checked every week in the United States and every 2 weeks in Canada throughout June and July 2011. All *A. planipennis* were collected, sexed, and summed for the entire field season. Catches of males, females, and total catch (males plus females) were analyzed separately for each experiment. Data from all experiments were transformed by log (x + 0.5) before being analyzed by randomized complete block design ANOVA. Tukey's honestly significant difference (HSD) test ($\alpha = 0.05$) was used to compare differences in catch for each sex between treatments.

At the low infested sites in Canada and the high level infested sites in the United States, the highest male catch was seen on green funnel traps baited with (3*Z*)-hexenol + (3*Z*)-lactone. No significant differences were seen in trap catch for males, females, or total (male + female) in either study.

Our results show that in low and medium/high infestation areas, dark green funnel traps coated with Rain-X® caught high numbers of *A. planipennis* with or without the presence of Manuka, (3*Z*)-hexenol, or (3*Z*)-lactone lures. At the release rate used, (3*Z*)-hexenol did appear to help increase male trap catch, but the differences were not significant. At the release rate used, the (3*Z*)-lactone lure improved male catch slightly (but not significantly) in both regions. Further testing of the (3*Z*)-lactone and (3*Z*)-hexenol at difference release rates on these traps is ongoing, along with further trap placement studies. It is hoped that this will optimize trap catch and further improve the detection rate of the current monitoring program effort for this insect.

Literature Cited

Bartelt, R.J.; Cossé, A.A.; Zilkowski, B.W.; Fraser, I. 2007. **Antennally active macrolide from the emerald ash borer, *Agrilus planipennis* emitted predominantly by females.** Journal of Chemical Ecology. 33: 1299–1302.

Crook, D.J.; Francese, J.A.; Zylstra, K.E.; Fraser, I.; Sawyer, A.J.; Bartels, D.W.; Lance, D.R.; Mastro, V.C. 2009. **Laboratory and field response of the emerald ash borer, *Agrilus planipennis* (Coleoptera: Buprestidae), to selected regions of the electromagnetic spectrum.** Journal of Economic Entomology. 102: 2160–2169.

Francese, J.A.; Crook, D.J.; Fraser, I.; Lance, D. R.; Sawyer, A.J.; Mastro, V.C. 2010. **Optimization of trap color for emerald ash borer (Coleoptera: Buprestidae).** Journal of Economic Entomology. 103(4): 1235-1241.

Francese, J.A.; Fraser, I.; Lance, D.R.; Mastro, V.C. 2011. **Efficacy of multifunnel traps for capturing emerald ash borer (Coleoptera: Buprestidae): effect of color, glue and other coatings.** Journal of Economic Entomology. 104 (3): 901-908.

Silk, P.J.; Ryall, K.; Mayo, P.; Lemay, M.A.; Grant, G.; Crook, D.J.; Cossé, A.; Fraser, I.; Sweeney, J.D.; Lyons, D.B.; Pitt, D.; Scarr, T.; Magee, D. 2011. **Evidence for a volatile pheromone in *Agrilus planipennis* Fairmaire (Coleoptera: Buprestidae) that increases attraction to a host foliar volatile.** Environmental Entomology. 40(4): 904-916.

THE EFFECT OF SOIL CA LEVELS ON MULTITROPHIC INTERACTIONS IN URBAN FORESTS INVADED BY *ROSA MULTIFLORA*: PROGRESS AS OF WINTER 2011-2012

Vincent D'Amico

U.S. Forest Service, Northern Research Station, Newark, DE 19713

ABSTRACT

Large-scale applications of calcium to forested watersheds damaged by acid deposition have been shown to have a number of beneficial effects on arthropod, gastropod, and bird populations (Pabian and Brittingham 2012). However, these studies have been conducted in larger unfragmented forests, relatively free of invasion by nonnative plant species. We established sites and collected data in 2010 and 2011 to explore these multitrophic relationships in highly fragmented and invaded forests.

Sites. Our study sites included 21 plots in deciduous forests in Delaware. Plots ranged in size from 2 to 16 hectares. The majority of the plots were sited in Newark city parks with others located on public city, county, or state properties (Fig. 1). All sites had at least one edge to standardize edge effects. In addition, plots were delineated in a grid pattern with orange wire stake flags placed every 25 meters. Numerical and alphabetical coordinates at each flag were used to determine location inside each plot.

Soil Sampling. Soil sampling occurred at 10 randomized flag locations for each field site location. In a randomized one square meter area around the flag, five soil core samples were taken from the top 10 cm of the soil. Core samples were mixed together to get a heterogeneous testable soil sample, were oven-dried for 72 hours, ground and sieved to 2 mm. Soil chemistry was determined through a variety of laboratory tests. The soil elements of particular interest were calcium, pH, and the calcium:aluminum ratio. If the calcium:aluminum ratio has a value greater than one, the soil has reached a threshold and is in the process of becoming less acidified.

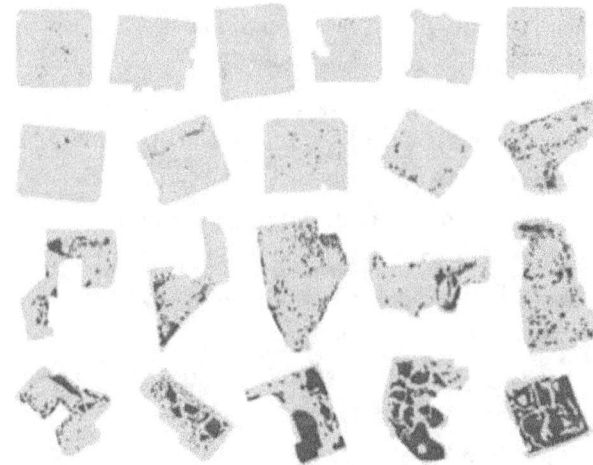

Figure 1.—Study sites in Delaware, with *R. multiflora*

Vegetation Sampling. Vegetation was sampled at the same randomized flag locations where soil, gastropod, and arthropod sampling occurred. Sampling of the plot vegetation composition occurred during July and August. The following vegetation variables were sampled: ground cover, shrub cover, tree basal area, vertical forest density, and total coarse woody debris. Nonnative plant species were recorded, with special effort to map the exact location of one of the most prevalent invasive plants, *Rosa multiflora*.

Arthropod Sampling. Arthropods were sampled at the same randomized flag locations where soil, vegetation, and gastropod sampling occurred. Litter was taken from 0.5 m^2 around the flag location. These litter samples were run through Berlese funnels and left for 3 days for the arthropods to collect in ethanol-filled jars. After the extraction of arthropods from the litter, the arthropods were counted and classified down to the level of family.

Gastropod Sampling. Terrestrial snails were sampled at the same randomized flag locations where soil, vegetation, and arthropod sampling occurred. Snails were sampled both by litter sieving and timed searches by two searchers for 10 minutes per flag. The number of snails and the species found during these searches were recorded. Snails were also sampled by litter sieving from the same litter collected during the arthropod sampling. After collection, the litter was dried, searched by hand, and examined for snails greater than 1 mm. These snails were counted and identified to the level of genus.

Avian Sampling. In order to determine the occupancy and territory density of our target bird species, we conducted spot map surveys throughout the field season. By marking bird activity on a site map during each visit, at the end of the season we were able to compile data to create a master map of territory locations for each species. We considered a territory to be established if we observed an individual male consistently singing in the same relative location in a 10 day period. These surveys were conducted 10 times a year over 3 years, with an average of 3 days between site visits. Active nests where the female was laying or feeding nestlings were monitored as they were found. To minimize nest disturbance, nests were checked every 2-5 days until nestlings fledged or failed. The numbers of eggs and/or young was recorded during these visits. Reproductive success was calculated for each species at each plot.

Sites were found to span a range of groundcover invasion by nonnative plants such as *R. multiflora* (Fig. 1). There was also a strong correlation with higher levels of available Ca and higher pH and the level of invadedness recorded. The percentage of multiflora rose shrubs at each flag point had a positive relationship with ionized soil calcium (linear regression, $r^2 = 0.05$, P = 0.002) as well as soil pH (linear regression: $r^2 = 0.05$, P = 0.001). We found that invertebrate abundance differed in relation to soil Ca availability as well (Fig. 2). Gastropods and crustaceans were positively associated with soil Ca, with snail abundance 2.4 time greater (F = 14.03, P < 0.001) in Ca-rich sites. In contrast, the overall abundance of insect taxa was negatively

associated with Ca. Insects may be negatively affected by increases in nonnative plant cover associated with high soil Ca levels, as the majority of insects sampled were herbivorous species. The extent of invasion by *R. multiflora* also affected the avian community. Wood thrush had a greater nest density in uninvaded sites while gray catbird had greater nest density in invaded sites (Fig. 3). At one site, invasion by *R. multiflora* continued to increase since 1966 and concurrently, wood thrush densities declined while catbird densities increased. We also found an interaction between *R. multiflora* cover, Ca:Al, and snail abundance. We conclude that in some cases, treatment of urban forest soils with Ca in the form of lime, whether intentionally or as a result of runoff from agricultural or privately owned property, could have the effect of increasing the degree of invasion by nonnative plants such as *R. multiflora*.

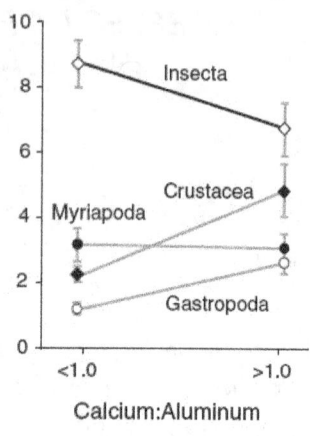

Figure 2.—Invertebrate abundance

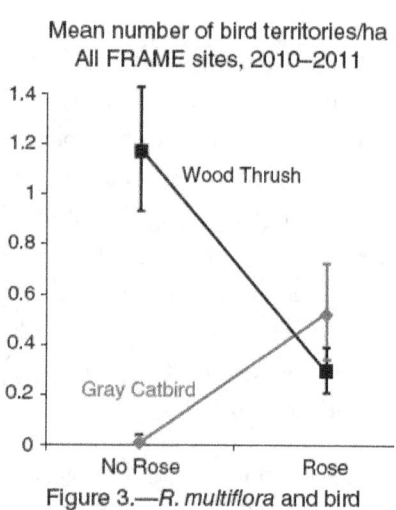

Figure 3.—*R. multiflora* and bird territories.

Literature Cited

Pabian, S.E.; Brittingham, M.C. 2011. **Soil calcium availability limits forest songbird productivity and density.** The Auk. 128: 441-447.

LARICOBIUS NIGRINUS ESTABLISHMENT, DISPERSAL, AND IMPACT ON HEMLOCK WOOLLY ADELGID (HWA) IN THE EASTERN UNITED STATES

Gina A. Davis[1], Scott M. Salom[2], Loke T. Kok[2], Carlyle C. Brewster[2], Brad Onken[3], and David Mausel[4]

[1]University of Massachusetts, Department of Plant, Soil, and Insect Sciences, Amherst, MA 01003
[2]Virginia Tech, Department of Entomology, Blacksburg, VA 24061
[3]U.S. Forest Service, Northeastern Area State and Private Forestry, Morgantown, WV 26505
[4]Menominee Tribal Enterprises, Neopit, WI 54150

ABSTRACT

Laricobius nigrinus Fender is native to western North America and is the most abundant predator observed in association with hemlock woolly adelgid (HWA), *Adelges tsugae* Annand. This predatory beetle was first released into the eastern United States in 2003 as part of a biological control program for an exotic invasion of HWA. According to the HWA Predator Release and Monitoring Database (Virginia Tech and USFS 2011), at least 154,000 beetles have been released across 15 states. The online tracking program contains data that are voluntarily entered by cooperators of the biological control program and may not contain all activities actually occurring in each state. Information within this database along with establishment and post-release studies provide direction to refine release and monitoring strategies for *L. nigrinus*.

Mausel et al. (2010) examined several factors that may influence the probability of establishment of *L. nigrinus* populations including HWA density, season of release, number of beetles released (75 to 1200), and minimum winter temperature at release sites. An established population was defined by the detection of at least the third generation. The probability of establishment increased as the number of beetles released increased and as minimum winter temperatures at release sites increased. Before 2010, the range of release size entered into the database also ranged from 75 to 1200 beetles, with an average release of 310 beetles at each site. In 2010, several releases of at least 2,000 beetles were made. Only 25 percent of the release sites entered into

the database had monitoring observations recorded for *L. nigrinus*. The predator was detected at 44 percent of those sites and at least the third generation was detected at 41 (32 percent) of the sites monitored.

Determining whether *L. nigrinus* establishes populations depends on our ability to detect small numbers of beetles in what is sometimes an expansive hemlock forest. The two primary sampling techniques for this predator are beat sheet sampling in the lower hemlock crowns for the adult life stage and cutting HWA-infested branches to rear immature life stages. Mausel et al. (2010) found that sampling only for the adult life stage can produce false negatives because even when no adults are found, larvae are often recovered at these same sites. Records in the database support this observation. When only the adult life stage was sampled, the results were negative at 60 percent of the sites; however when both the adult and larval life stages were sampled, negative results were obtained at only 7 percent of the monitored sites.

Understanding predator dispersal would also help to guide release and monitoring strategies. Vertical dispersal of *L. nigrinus* within a tree and horizontal dispersal between hemlocks were examined for 2 years after the release of 300 adults at four locations, including two in central Pennsylvania and two in southwest Virginia. The density of HWA was moderate to high in the three crown strata (< 7, 7-15, > 15 m) of release trees sampled for the first generation of

L. nigrinus, with 88 percent of the larvae recovered above 7 m in the crown. The following year, HWA was difficult to find on the release trees in Pennsylvania, which prevented sampling for the vertical movement of *L. nigrinus*. However, 98 percent of the second generation collected at the sites in Virginia was above 7 m. Monitoring for horizontal dispersal was only carried out in the lower crowns of release trees and on infested hemlocks at increasing distances from the release trees. A single F_1 larva was detected 10 m from a release tree in Pennsylvania; in the following year, when HWA populations were sparse on the release trees, F_2 larvae were detected at a maximum of 50 m. This was in contrast to Virginia where the maximum distance from release trees was only 10 m for the F_2 generation. The distribution of *L. nigrinus* within a 10-hectare area surrounding sites where the predator had previously established populations was evaluated at four sites, including two where 300 beetles and two where 600 beetles were released. In 2008, a greater proportion of the fourth and fifth generation larvae were recovered closer to the release areas, regardless of HWA density. By the fifth and sixth generations, the number of larvae detected was no longer correlated with distance but was positively correlated with the density of HWA. Combining the observations made at both the new release and established sites, we estimated the spread rate for *L. nigrinus* at 39 m/year. This rate is a conservative estimate based on observations made within a restricted range from the release area.

An initial examination of *L. nigrinus* impact on HWA was made by comparing observations on release trees with geographically separated control trees at paired sites in Pennsylvania and North Carolina. Predation and HWA survival were measured on branch samples from the lower crowns of five trees at the four sites. Observations were made for 4 consecutive years and spanned 3 to 7 years after *L. nigrinus* release. The density of both the prey and predator fluctuated annually at both sites, and the number of *L. nigrinus* maintained a positive correlation with HWA density. We did not detect suppression of HWA populations, as there was no significant difference between HWA survival on release and control trees. However, there was a trend of reduced HWA survival on the release trees each year. This study concluded just 6 and 7 years after 600 *L. nigrinus* were released on the most heavily infested hemlocks within the stand. A possible bias in the experimental design was that observations were only on the release trees which may not represent predation on HWA in the surrounding hemlock stand. Alternatively, we must consider that more time is probably needed for relatively small predator population releases to increase in size and to have a measurable effect on HWA populations.

The research presented here along with the work of many others has contributed valuable information to refine the HWA biological control program and its long-term assessment. Some of the refinements include more stringent site selection criteria that focus efforts on relatively healthy hemlock stands with low to moderate HWA infestations. Release sizes are being increased with some large-scale releases of 4,000 or more beetles, and existing release sites are being augmented with additional beetles. These efforts are made possible by successful laboratory rearing programs, redistributing *L. nigrinus* from highly productive release sites, and direct collections in coastal Washington and northern Idaho. We have also improved post-release monitoring efforts by understanding *L. nigrinus* dispersal behavior. After monitoring six generations of *L. nigrinus,* we found that this predator was slow to disperse from an abundant source of food, and that it was capable of locating isolated HWA-infested hemlocks. The key is to sample the most heavily infested hemlocks and recognize that monitoring only for the adult life stage or within the lower crowns may not be sensitive enough to detect small populations of *L. nigrinus*.

It was promising that *L. nigrinus* persisted on release trees, but long-term assessments should evaluate hemlocks throughout the stand and consider variability of HWA within the crown. Predation can be evaluated annually by comparing release and control stands or using caged branch comparisons. To distinguish any regulatory role of the biological control agents from other biotic or abiotic factors, we should begin to build full life tables for HWA in the presence of the introduced agents. Biological control remains the primary management option to maintain the health of hemlock forests, and it is likely that multiple species are needed to suppress HWA. Integrating what we have learned about *L. nigrinus* with studies of HWA biology, hemlock defenses, and interactions with the elongate hemlock scale is needed for a holistic management program that considers the complexity of the entire hemlock system.

Literature Cited

Virginia Tech and U.S. Department of Agriculture, Forest Service. 2011. **HWA predator release and monitoring database**. Available at http://hwa.ento.vt.edu/hwa/hwa.cgi. (Accessed December 20, 2011).

Mausel, D.L.; Salom, S.M.; Kok, L.T.; Davis, G.A. 2010. **Establishment of the hemlock woolly adelgid predator, *Laricobius nigrinus* (Coleoptera: Derodontidae), in the Eastern United States**. Journal of Environmental Entomology. 39: 440-448.

TRAPPING OF EUROPEAN OAK BUPRESTID SPECIES USING VISUAL AND OLFACTORY CUES

Michael J. Domingue[1], Gyuri Csoka[2], Miklos Toth[3], Zoltan Imrei[3], Jonathan P. Lelito[4], Victor C. Mastro[5], and Thomas C. Baker[1]

[1]Pennsylvania State University, Chemical Ecology Laboratory, University Park, PA 16802
[2]Hungarian Forest Research Institute, Matrafured Hungary
[3]Plant Protection Institute, Hungarian Academy of Sciences, Budapest, Hungary
[4]USDA APHIS, PPQ, Brighton MI 48116
[5]USDA APHIS, PPQ, Buzzards Bay, MA 02542

ABSTRACT

We applied a variety of techniques developed for trapping *Agrilus planipennis* Fairmaire in an effort to capture other *Agrilus* species found in European oak forests. These species included *Agrilus sulcicollis*, a recently detected exotic pest in North America (Haack et al. 2009), as well as *Agrilus biguttatus*, a more aggressive pest that is known to kill trees within its native range (Moraal and Hilszczanski 2000). The behaviors that we attempted to evoke included the visual mating approaches first observed for *A. planipennis* (Lelito et al. 2007) but also observed for several *Agrilus* species, including the oak-feeding species of interest (Domingue et al. 2011). We baited traps with chemical formulations of tree-produced volatiles such as Manuka oil and (Z)-3-hexen-1-ol, which have been shown to be attractive to *A. planipennis* (Crook et al 2008, de Groot et al. 2008). We also used fly lures consisting of Z9-tricosene, which is similar to *A. planipennis* cuticular hydrocarbons such as Z9-tricosane, which has been shown to be a contact pheromone.

Novel sticky traps were devised that rested over the leaves in the canopy. These traps provided parallel surfaces that slope slightly downward away from each other. In one experiment exploring the optimum visual characteristics of such traps, the following materials were used on the surfaces: 1) green plastic, 2) purple plastic, 3) cut leaves, or 4) no covering (white cardboard surface). In each case, the traps were either provided with *A. planipennis* visual decoy baits to evoke male visual mating approaches or left blank. The traps were then covered with Tanglefoot®. These traps were compared to simple preparations of Tanglefoot® directly applied to leaves in situ, with or without beetle decoys. Another experiment was performed with odor dispensers including either: 1) Manuka oil, 2) (Z)-3-hexen-1-ol, 3) Z9-tricosene, or 4) no odor. Green or purple plastic-covered traps, with and without decoy beetles, were employed within 0.5 m of each lure. Sticky leaves with and without visual decoys were also prepared within 0.5 m of each lure.

In the first visual trap characteristic experiment, a total of 483 *Agrilus* beetles were caught in 12 traps. Three of these beetles (0.6 percent) were *A. biguttatus*, while 16 percent were *A. sulcicollis*. The green plastic-covered traps performed most efficiently with a mean (± S.E.) of 2.7±0.7 total *Agrilus* captured per day without a visual decoy and 4.2±0.7 *Agrilus* per day with a visual decoy. All other trap designs were much less effective.

The second experiment, which involved odor lures, led to the capture of 1462 *Agrilus* beetles in 128 traps. Similarly, only 10 (0.7 percent) were *A. biguttatus* while 13 percent were *A. sulcicollis*. Again, the green plastic-covered traps were much more effective than the purple plastic-covered traps or the sticky leaf traps, capturing 1.9±0.3 beetles per day without decoys or 2.5±0.3 beetles per day with decoys.

Of the 13 *A. biguttatus* captures observed in both experiments, all but one were on either green plastic traps (9) or sticky leaves (3), and 11 of these traps had *A. planipennis* visual decoys. The remaining trap catching this species was a white trap with a visual decoy. Because equal numbers of decoy-baited versus unbaited traps were deployed, the effect of the decoy on *A. biguttatus* capture was highly significant ($X^2 = 9.3$, d.f. = 1, p = 0.002).

From this experiment, we determined that our green plastic traps are an effective and inexpensive tool for detecting multiple *Agrilus* species in a forest setting. Both odor lures and visual decoys increase captures, but further research is needed to determine which blends of odors might provide optimal capture rates. The visual decoys were especially important for *A. biguttatus*, which was only detected once on a trap without a decoy. Further research envisions refinement of the physical characteristics of the traps, as well as calibration of the efficiency of these small economical traps with established detection tools such as prism traps.

Literature Cited

Crook, D.J.; Khrimian, A.; Fraser, I.; Francese, J.A.; Poland, T.M.; Mastro, V.C. 2008. **Electrophysiological and behavioral responses of *Agrilus planipennis* (Coleoptera: Buprestidae) to host bark volatiles.** Environmental Entomology. 37: 356–365.

de Groot, P.; Grant, G.G.; Poland, T.M.; Scharbach, R.; Buchan, L.; Nott, R.W.; Macdonald, L.; Pitt, D. 2008. **Electrophysiological response and attraction of emerald ash borer to green leaf volatiles (GLVs) emitted by host foliage.** Journal of Chemical Ecology. 34: 1170–1179.

Domingue, M.J.; Csóka, G.; Tóth, M.; Vétek, G.; Pénzes, B.; Mastro, V.; Baker, T.C. 2011. **Field observations of visual attraction of three European oak buprestid beetles toward conspecific and heterospecific models.** Entomologia Experimentalis et Applicata. 140(2): 112–121.

Haack, R.A.; Petrice, T.R.; Zablotny, J.E. 2009. **First report of the European oak borer, *Agrilus sulcicollis* (Coleoptera: Buprestidae), in the United States.** Great Lakes Entomologist. 42: 1-7.

Lelito, J.P.; Fraser, I.; Mastro, V.C.; Tumlinson, J.H.; Boroczky, K.; Baker, T.C. 2007. **Visually mediated "paratrooper copulations" in the mating behavior of *Agrilus planipennis* (Coleoptera: Buprestidae), a highly destructive invasive pest of North American ash trees.** Journal of Insect Behavior. 20: 537–552.

Moraal, L.G.; Hilszczanski, J. 2000. **The oak buprestid beetle, *Agrilus biguttatus* (F.) (Coleoptera: Buprestidae), a recent factor in oak decline in Europe.** Journal of Pest Science. 73: 134-138.

RECENT PROGRESS IN BIOLOGICAL CONTROL OF EMERALD ASH BORER IN NORTH AMERICA

Jian J. Duan[1], Leah S. Bauer[2], Juli Gould[3], Jonathan P. Lelito[4], and Roy Van Driesche[5]

[1]USDA ARS, Beneficial Insects Introduction Research Unit, Newark, DE 19713
[2]U.S. Forest Service, Northern Research Station, East Lansing, MI 48823
[3]USDA APHIS, PPQ, CPHST, Buzzards Bay, MA 02542
[4]USDA APHIS, PPQ, Brighton, MI 48116
[5]University of Massachusetts, Department of Plant, Soil and Insect
Sciences, Amherst, MA 01003

ABSTRACT

Since the emerald ash borer (EAB), *Agrilus planipennis* Fairmaire, was first discovered near Detroit, MI in 2002, infestations have been found in a total of 15 U.S. states and 2 Canadian provinces, threatening the existence of North American ash trees (*Fraxinus* spp.). Immediately following the discovery of EAB, researchers began studying EAB natural enemies in the United States and China. Five years later, researchers started introducing three species of hymenopteran parasitoids from China and known to attack EAB in its native home of China: *Spathius agrili* (Braconidae), *Tetrastichus planipennis* (Eulophidae), and *Oobius agrili* (Encyrtidae). The first two parasitoid species attack late-instar EAB larvae, and *O. agrili* attacks EAB eggs. Two years later, the U.S. Department of Agriculture Animal and Plant Health Inspection Service (USDA APHIS) completed construction and staffed the EAB Biological Control Rearing Facility, and now large numbers of these introduced parasitoids are being reared there. These parasitoids have been released at field sites in 12 EAB-infested states. As of fall 2011, we have confirmed that these introduced Chinese parasitoids successfully established in at least five states (Michigan, Maryland, Ohio, Illinois, and Indiana), although their combined impacts on EAB population growth are still not known. It is hopeful that populations of these EAB parasitoids will continue to expand and exert significant control of EAB populations within the next few years in the United States.

Additional foreign exploration conducted by the USDA researchers and collaborators in the Russian Far East (near Vladivostok) resulted in the discovery of two additional Asiatic braconids attacking EAB larvae (*Spathius galinae* and *Atanycolus picipes*) as well as one encyrtid egg parasitoid (genus and species to be described). These three Russian parasitoids were imported to the USDA quarantine facilities and are being tested against nontarget woodborers to assess their host specificity and identify any possible nontarget effects. Climatic matching indicates that parasitoids from the Russian Far East are potentially more cold tolerant than ones sourced from China (especially *S. agrili*) and should be considered for introduction to the northeast United States for biological control of EAB.

In addition to the aforementioned classical biological control efforts, extensive surveys of indigenous natural enemies have also been conducted in the United States. Currently, several indigenous hymenopteran parasitoids have been discovered attacking larvae of EAB in Michigan, Pennsylvania, Maryland, and Ohio. The role of these indigenous parasitoids in suppressing EAB population growth and EAB spread in North America is not clear since the EAB parasitism by these species is generally low. However, one group of North American native braconids (*Atanycolus* spp.) in Michigan has been found to cause high (>50 percent) levels of parasitism in some locations where EAB populations are very high and damaging to host trees. Extensive field investigations into the potential role of both introduced and indigenous natural enemies in suppressing EAB population growth and spread has been under way in both the epicenter of EAB infestation (Michigan) and newly infested areas (Maryland and New York). The introduction and establishment of parasitoids from the native home of EAB (China and Russia) will likely continue to be a critical component of the current EAB management strategies in North America.

ASIAN LONGHORNED BEETLE DETECTOR DOG PILOT PROJECT

Monica Errico

USDA APHIS, PPQ, PDC National Detector Dog Training Center, Newnan, GA 30265

ABSTRACT

The first confirmed infestation of the Asian Longhorned Beetle (ALB), *Anoplophora glabripennis,* was in 1996. The beetle is believed to have been brought into the United States in cargo shipments from China. Currently, detection of ALB infestations relies on visual inspections from the ground or with tree climbers along with testing of traps and lures. Trees that are identified as being positive are removed, and potential host trees in the area are treated with insecticides. These methods of eradication can be both labor intensive and expensive to implement. Utilizing detector dogs would benefit the emergency response effort by improving the ability to detect early infestations in an easier and timely manner. This would allow resources such as ground crews and traps to be allocated to the targeted areas based on the canine responses, potentially shortening the timeline to eradication.

Canines were trained to detect and respond to ALB using frass from the insect. Initial training was conducted inside regulated areas during pre-emergence using infested material, known positive trees, and areas which contained many ALB infested trees. Canines were trained to search for potential targets at the base of the tree, in branches on the ground, and under the canopy of trees. We are currently training on firewood using wood lots as well as the outside perimeters of impermeable areas.

Three detector dogs, two Labrador retriever mixes and one beagle, were chosen based on their breed traits, characteristics, and search strategies. Observations of trends and patterns are being noted to determine their overall abilities and capabilities of utilization.

Proficiency trials were conducted in controlled environments. The trials were double blind, and neither the handler nor dog knew where the target odor was located. The detector dogs were 80-90 percent successful in their ability to detect and respond to ALB frass. Following successful completion of the trials, dog teams were utilized for surveys in Worcester, MA. In August 2011, the canine teams conducted their first survey of approximately 5 acres containing 19 host trees that ranged in height from 21-45 feet tall with dense canopies. Canine teams were able to survey the area in approximately 20 minutes and responded to five trees which were later identified as being positive for ALB infestation. In September 2011, we returned to Worcester to survey areas around traps that had caught live beetles. While surveying a unit (block) in a residential neighborhood, the dogs detected another ALB infested area.

Detector dogs have proven they can be an effective, efficient survey tool to locate ALB infestations. Canines are also capable of conducting surveys of larger areas which would increase the number of inspections performed in a shorter period of time. In addition, canine teams can be ambassadors and outreach tool for any eradication program.

EVALUATION OF HYBRIDIZATION AMONG THREE LARICOBIUS SPP. PREDATORS OF HEMLOCK WOOLLY ADELGID (ADELGIDAE): PRELIMINARY RESULTS

Melissa Joy Fischer[1], Nathan P. Havill[2], Gina A. Davis[3], Scott M. Salom[1], and Loke T. Kok[1]

[1]Virginia Tech, Department of Entomology, VA 24061
[2]U.S. Forest Service, Northern Research Station, Hamden, CT 06514
[3]University of Massachusetts, Department of Plant, Soil and Insect Science, Amherst, MA 01003

ABSTRACT

Laricobius spp. (Coleoptera: Derodontidae) feed exclusively on Adelgidae. Consequently, this genus has gained attention as potential biocontrol agents of hemlock woolly adelgid (HWA), *Adelges tsugae* Annand, an invasive insect from Japan that has caused extensive mortality of eastern and Carolina hemlock (*Tsuga canadensis* (L.) Carr. and *Tsuga caroliniana* Engelm). *Laricobius nigrinus* Fender, a predator of HWA from the Pacific Northwest and Canada, has been released as a biocontrol agent in the eastern United States since 2003. *Laricobius osakensis* Montgomery and Shiyake from Japan is being considered for release as an additional biocontrol agent of HWA.

In 2009, it was confirmed that *L. nigrinus* was hybridizing with *Laricobius rubidus* LeConte. *Laricobius rubidus* is native to the east coast and feeds primarily on pine bark adelgid (PBA), *Pineus strobi* Hartig. Hybridization between the two species may affect biocontrol efforts against HWA or the relationship *L. rubidus* has in regulating PBA. Hybridization may have a negative impact on biocontrol efforts against HWA if the hybrids are less fit than their parents via processes such as the sterility of the F_1 or F_2 generation or outbreeding depression. Both scenarios could lower the fitness of the species through reduced reproductive output. Hybridization could also positively impact biocontrol efforts if hybrids are more fit than their parents via new gene combinations that result in better adaptation to the ecological niche that HWA provides.

Hybrids with greater fitness than the parental species could have a negative effect on the ability of *L. rubidus* to regulate PBA if hybrids displace *L. rubidus* at the sites where they are both present. Due to these potential effects, it is important to determine how hybridization between *L. rubidus* and *L. nigrinus* will transpire and to determine if *L. osakensis* is capable of hybridizing with *L. nigrinus* and/or *L. rubidus* before it is released.

The objectives of this study were to: (1) determine if *L. nigrinus* and *L. osakensis* are capable of mating and producing viable progeny, and (2) use genetic markers to determine if hybridization between *L. rubidus* and *L. nigrinus* is occurring at all sites used in the study, how hybridization is changing over time, and the host preference of hybrids in a natural setting.

Laricobius osakensis and *L. nigrinus* were found to be capable of mating and ovipositing fertile eggs, but the eggs were not viable. A no-choice mating experiment showed that with no choice of mate, fecundity (the number of eggs produced) was significantly lower for the interspecific cross (*L. nigrinus* x *L. osakensis*) compared with one intraspecific cross (*L. osakensis* x *L. osakensis*) in 2010 and two intraspecific crosses (*L. osakensis* x *L. osakensis* and *L. nigrinus* x *L. nigrinus*) in 2011. When presented with a choice of mate, there was no significant difference in the number of progeny produced between intra- and interspecific crosses.

A field study determined that hybridization between *L. nigrinus* and *L. rubidus* is not occurring at all sites (6 out of 10 sites in 2010). Three sites that had been examined for the occurrence of hybridization from 2007 through 2010 were found to have a decrease in percent hybridization. A significant positive relationship was found between percent hybridization and the number of years since *L. nigrinus* was released at the sites. In 2010, sampling from hemlock and white pine in the field revealed that *L. nigrinus* is most often associated with HWA, *L. rubidus* is associated with both PBA and HWA, and hybrids are most often associated with HWA. Because *L. nigrinus* and the hybrids are found almost exclusively on HWA, hybridization does not currently appear to be negatively affecting the HWA biocontrol program. Whether hybridization is impacting the relationship *L. rubidus* has in regulating PBA is inconclusive.

DEVELOPING AN IMPROVED TRAPPING TOOL TO SURVEY CERAMBYCID BEETLES: EVALUATION OF TRAP HEIGHT AND LURE COMPOSITION

Elizabeth E. Graham[1], Therese M. Poland[1,2], Deborah G. McCullough[2], and Jocelyn G. Miller[3]

[1]Michigan State University, Department of Entomology, East Lansing, MI 48824
[2]U.S. Forest Service, Northern Research Station, East Lansing, MI 48823
[3]University of California, Department of Entomology, Riverside, CA 92521

ABSTRACT

Wood-boring beetles in the family Cerambycidae (Coleoptera) play important roles in many forest ecosystems. However, an increasing number of species are invading new countries via international commerce, and some of these exotic species threaten forest health in North America and globally (Brockerhoff et al. 2006, Nowak et al. 2001, Paine et al. 1995). At high densities, larvae of these beetles can damage and kill trees in natural forests, urban forests, plantations, and orchards, and degrade lumber by infesting saw logs (Allison et al. 2004, Solomon 1995). Nonnative cerambycids represent a substantial threat because they are easily transported as larvae or pupae within the wood of dunnage and other packing materials, and such materials have been identified as a major pathway for introducing exotic wood borers (Brockerhoff et al. 2006, Haack 2006). In addition, both larvae and adult beetles can infest firewood, nursery stock, and a variety of imported commodities (McCullough et al. 2006).

In the past decade, a handful of semiochemicals have been identified as pheromones for several species. Some of these compounds such as 3R-hydroxyketone, 2R,3R-(2,3) hexanediol, fuscumol, and fuscumol acetate are conserved within the subfamilies, and multiple species will respond to the same lure (Hanks et al. 2007, Mitchell et al. 2011). Because multiple species respond to these compounds, they are well suited to be used for surveying stand composition and monitoring for potential pest species. Blending these different compounds into one single lure would eliminate the need for multiple traps and save researchers time and money. The effect of combining these compounds into one "super" lure has not been tested across a vertical gradient. Combining the pheromones could inhibit the response to individual compounds.

Our goal was to identify effective detection tools for a broad array of cerambycid species by first testing different traps types (in 2010) and then using the most effective trap type to test known cerambycid pheromones released alone and in combination (in 2011). We compared numbers and species richness of cerambycid beetles captured with flight intercept traps placed either at base level (1.5 m high) or canopy level (~3-10 m high) in hardwood and conifer sites.

Our study conducted in the summer of 2010 compared trap type and height at four different site classifications: hardwood forest, conifer forest, wooded area adjacent to an industrial site, and wooded area adjacent to a residential site. We compared two types of traps, cross-vane panel traps (AlphaScents, Portland, OR) and 12-unit Lindgren multiple-funnel traps (Contech Enterprises, Inc., Delta, B.C., Canada), located at the base level and the canopy level to determine the most effective combination for capturing cerambycid beetles. We captured 3,723 beetles representing 72 cerambycid species from June 10 to July 15, 2010. Overall, the cross-vane panel traps captured approximately 1.5 times more beetles than funnel traps. Twenty-one species were captured exclusively in traps at one height, either in the canopy or at base level. The most species (59) were captured in hardwood sites where a greater diversity of host material was available compared to conifer (34 species), residential (41 species), or industrial (49) sites. Cross-vane panel traps installed across a vertical gradient should maximize the number of cerambycid species captured.

We conducted a second study in 2011 to determine the most efficient lure or combination of lures for capturing a wide diversity of cerambycid beetles and compared the composition of cerambycid beetles captured at the ground and canopy level. We sampled communities of Cerambycidae from June 7 to August 12, 2011 using paired cross-vane panel traps set at base level and canopy level at six different sites in Michigan. Each site contained two blocks of traps with each block comprised of one of the following lures: host volatile blend (ethanol + α-pinene + ipsenol), the racemic blends of 3-hydroxyhexan-2-one, 2R,3R-(2,3) hexanediol, 2-undecyloxy-1-ethanol, (E)-6,10-dimethyl-5,9-undecadien-2-ol, its acetate, a blend of the five pheromones, and a blank. We captured a total of 8,214 beetles from 97 species of Cerambycidae in six subfamilies. The host volatile blend and the pheromone blend captured significantly more species per trap and the greatest number of species overall compared to the individual pheromones. Traps baited with the host volatile blend captured a total of 61 species, with 50 species captured in the traps located at the base level and 47 species captured in traps located at the canopy. Traps baited with the pheromone blend also captured a total of 61 species, with 47 species caught in base level traps and 47 captured in canopy level traps. The species composition of the canopy traps different from the species composition of the base traps. Traps baited with the individual pheromones captured 29 species that were not captured in traps baited with the pheromone blend and 32 species that were not captured in traps baited with the host volatile blend. Seven of the 13 most abundant species responded to traps baited with the pheromone blend in significantly lower numbers

than traps baited with a single pheromone, suggesting that the pheromone blend may inhibit some species. Species richness, diversity, and evenness were lower in the conifer sites. Eleven species were captured exclusively at conifer sites and 24 species were captured exclusively at hardwood sites. The results of this study reinforce the need to trap across a vertical gradient. The blend of pheromones works well for surveying the abundant species in a forest; however it should not be used for detecting newly established or rare species because a component of the blend could possibly inhibit the response of that species.

Literature Cited

Allison, J.D.; Borden, J.H.; Seybold, S.J. 2004. **A review of the chemical ecology of the Cerambycidae (Coleoptera).** Chemoecology. 14: 123-150.

Brockerhoff, E.G.; Liebhold, A.M.; Jactel, H. 2006. **The ecology of forest insect invasions and advances in their management.** Canadian Journal of Forest Research. 36: 263-268.

Haack, R.A. 2006. **Exotic bark- and wood-boring Coleoptera in the United States: recent establishments and interceptions**. Canadian Journal of Forest Research. 36: 269-288.

Hanks, L.M.; Millar, J.G.; Moreira, J.A.; Barbour, J.D.; Lacey, E.S.; McElfresh, J.S.; Reuter, F.R.; Ray. A.M. 2007. **Using generic pheromone lures to expedite identification of aggregation pheromones for the cerambycid beetles, *Xylotrechus nauticus*, *Phymatodes lecontei*, and *Neoclytus modestus modestus*.** Journal of Chemical Ecology. 33: 889-907.

McCullough, D.G.; Work, T.T.; Cavey, J.F.; Liebhold, A.M.; Marshall, D. 2006. **Interceptions of nonindigenous plant pests at US ports of entry and border crossings over a 17-year period.** Biological Invasions. 8: 611-630.

Mitchell, R.F.; Graham, E.E.; Wong, J.C.H.; Reagel, P.F.; Striman, B.L.; Hughes, G.P.; Paschen, M.A.; Ginzel, M.D.; Millar, J.G.; Hanks. L.M. 2011. **Fuscumol and fuscumol acetate are general attractants for many species of cerambycid beetles in the subfamily Lamiinae.** Entomologia Experimentalis et Applicata. 141: 71-77.

Nowak, D.J.; Pasek, J.E.; Sequeira, R.A.; Crane, D.E.; Mastro, V.C. 2001. **Potential effect of Anoplophora glabripennis (Coleoptera: Cerambycidae) on urban trees in the United States.** Journal of Economic Entomology. 94: 116-122.

Paine, T.D.; Millar, J.G.; Hanks, L.M. 1995. **Biology of the eucalyptus longhorned borer in California and development of an integrated management program for the urban forest.** California Agriculture. 49 (Jan.-Feb.): 34-37.

Solomon, J.D. 1995. **Guide to insect borers in North American broadleaf trees and shrubs.** Agriculture Handbook 706. Washington, DC: U.S. Department of Agriculture, Forest Service. 735 p.

CHALLENGES IN ASSESSING THE EFFECTIVENESS OF INTERNATIONAL AND DOMESTIC TREATMENTS FOR WOOD PACKAGING AND FIREWOOD

Robert A. Haack and Toby R. Petrice

U.S. Forest Service, Northern Research Station, East Lansing, MI 48823

ABSTRACT

Numerous nonnative bark- and wood-infesting insects have become established in countries outside their native range during the past century. Although the exact pathway by which each exotic borer was moved to a new country is seldom known, because of their cryptic life style, most were likely transported in wood packaging material (WPM) including pallets and crating associated with international trade (Haack 2006, Haack et al. 2010a). Once established in a new country, exotic borers spread both naturally and by human-assisted dispersal such as through the movement of infested firewood (Haack et al. 2010b). This presentation covered background information on international efforts to reduce the spread of insect pests in WPM and U.S. domestic efforts to reduce the movement of exotic borers in firewood.

In 2002, the international community responded to the phytosanitary risk posed by untreated WPM by approving International Standards for Phytosanitary Measures No. 15 (ISPM 15), which is entitled "International standards for phytosanitary measures: guidelines for regulating wood packaging material in international trade" (IPPC 2002). The original goal of ISPM 15 was to "practically eliminate the risk for most quarantine pests and significantly reduce the risk from a number of other pests that may be associated" with WPM (IPPC 2002). New Zealand was the first to implement ISPM 15 in 2003, followed by Australia in 2004, and the European Union in 2005. The United States did not fully implement ISPM 15 until 2006. As of today, over 70 countries have implemented ISPM 15 and several other countries are in the process of implementing it.

Since 2002, heat treatment and methyl bromide fumigation have been the only approved phytosanitary treatments for WPM. An additional method of heat treating wood described as dielectric heating (DH) will be available soon and includes both microwave and radio-frequency heating. To date, ISPM 15 has been revised twice, first in 2006 and again in 2009. Some key changes made in these revisions include lengthening the fumigation time from 16 to 24 hours, requiring the use of debarked wood for WPM with debarking preceding fumigation, and placing size limits on any single piece or residual bark (<50 cm^2) (Haack and Petrice 2009; IPPC 2006, 2009).

In recent years, many groups have been curious about how effective ISPM 15 has been in reducing the incidence of live insects in WPM. One such group is sponsored by The Nature Conservancy through the National Center for Ecological Analysis and Synthesis (NCEAS) at the University of California–Santa Barbara and is entitled "Effects of Trade Policy on Management of NonNative Forest Pests and Pathogens" (Brockerhoff et al. 2011). Results from this group have not yet been published, but the aim of one study was to locate and compare WPM infestation rates pre- and post-ISPM 15. Overall, few datasets were found worldwide, and they were not easily comparable (Bulman 1992, 1998; Haack and Petrice 2009; Zahid et al. 2008). This emphasizes the importance of collecting comparable data both before and after implementation of major international phytosanitary regulations so that the impact of the new policy can be assessed. Given that more ISPMs are expected in the future (e.g., plants for planting), appropriate preimplementation data should be collected now so that policy effectiveness can be assessed in the future.

It is important to recognize that many factors can influence the incidence of live borers in WPM after treatment. For example, some borers could survive the treatment, some could infest the WPM after treatment, some treatment facilities could be using equipment that is defective or improperly calibrated, and there is always the possibility of fraud (Haack and Brockerhoff 2011, Haack and Petrice 2009).

An update was also provided on recent decisions by the U.S. Department of Agriculture Animal and Plant Health Inspection Service (USDA APHIS) and various research findings related to wood pest movement in WPM and firewood. For example, in 2011, USDA APHIS published a risk assessment for the movement of domestic WPM within the United States (USDA APHIS 2011a). APHIS subsequently decided not to regulate domestic WPM and would not require domestic WPM to be treated to ISPM-15 standards. In addition, USDA APHIS used recent research findings (Myers et al. 2009) to justify a reduction in the heat treatment schedule from 71 °C for 75 min to 60 °C for 60 min for intrastate movement of domestic hardwood firewood to areas outside the quarantine zone for emerald ash borer, *Agrilus planipennis* Fairmaire (USDA APHIS 2011b). Research findings were presented indicating that heat-treating ash bolts to a minimum core temperature of 56 °C for 30 minutes resulted in 100 percent mortality of emerald ash borer prepupae (Haack and Petrice, unpublished data). Highlights were also presented on a survey for wood borers in firewood confiscated from vehicles that crossed the Mackinac Bridge between Michigan's upper and lower peninsulas (Haack et al. 2010b). Of the 1045 pieces of firewood representing 21 tree genera that were inspected, 23 percent of the firewood pieces were infested with live borers and another 41 percent had signs of prior borer infestation. In addition, for 322 surveys with drivers who dropped off firewood, 83 percent stated that their firewood originated from Michigan, while the others said that their firewood originated from 17 other U.S. states and 3 Canadian provinces.

Literature Cited

Brockerhoff, E.G.; Aukema, J.E.; Britton, K.O.; Cavey, J.F.; Garrett, L.J.; Haack, R.A.; Kimberley, M.; Liebhold, A.M.; Lowenstein, F.L.; Marasas, C.; Nuding, A.; Olson, L.; Speekmann, C.; Springborn, M.; Vieglais, C.; Turner, J. 2011. **Demonstrating the benefits of phytosanitary regulations: the case of ISPM 15.** In: McManus, K.A.; Gottschalk, K.W., eds. Proceedings, 21st U.S. Department of Agriculture interagency research forum on invasive species 2010. Gen. Tech. Rep. NRS-P-75. Newtown Square, PA: U.S. Department of Agriculture, Forest Service, Northern Research Station: 6-7.

Bulman, L.S. 1992. **Forestry quarantine risk of cargo imported into New Zealand.** New Zealand Journal of Forestry Science. 22: 32-38.

Bulman, L.S. 1998. **Quarantine risk posed to forestry container loads, and efficiency of FCL door inspections.** New Zealand Journal of Forestry Science. 28: 335-346.

Haack, R.A. 2006. **Exotic bark and wood-boring Coleoptera in the United States: recent establishments and interceptions.** Canadian Journal of Forest Research. 36: 269-288.

Haack R.A.; Brockerhoff, E.G. 2011. **ISPM No. 15 and the incidence of wood pests: recent findings, policy changes, and current knowledge gaps.** International Research Group on Wood Protection 42nd Annual Meeting; 5-8 May 2011; Queenstown, New Zealand. Stockholm, Sweden: IRG Secretariat. IRG/WP 11-30568. Available at http://www.treesearch.fs.fed.us/pubs/39922. [Date accessed unknown].

Haack, R.A.; Hérard, F.; Sun, J.; Turgeon, J.J. 2010a. **Managing invasive populations of Asian longhorned beetle and citrus longhorned beetle: a worldwide perspective.** Annual Review of Entomology. 55: 521–546

Haack, R.A.; Petrice, T.R. 2009. **Bark- and wood-borer colonization of logs and lumber after heat treatment to ISPM 15 specifications: the role of residual bark.** Journal of Economic Entomology. 102: 1075-1084.

Haack R.A.; Petrice, T.R.; Wiedenhoeft, A.C. 2010b. **Incidence of bark- and wood-boring insects in firewood: a survey at Michigan's Mackinac Bridge.** Journal of Economic Entomology. 103: 1682-1692.

International Plant Protection Convention (IPPC). 2002. **International standards for phytosanitary measures: guidelines for regulating wood packaging material in international trade.** Publ. No. 15. Rome, Italy: Food and Agriculture Organization of the United Nations.

International Plant Protection Convention (IPPC). 2006. **International standards for phytosanitary measures: ISPM 15-guidelines for regulating wood packaging material in international trade with modifications to annex I.** Rome, Italy: Food and Agriculture Organization of the United Nations.

International Plant Protection Convention (IPPC). 2009. **International standards for phytosanitary measures: revision of ISPM 15-regulation of wood packaging material in international trade.** Rome, Italy: Food and Agriculture Organization of the United Nations.

Myers, S.W.; Fraser, I.; Mastro; V.C. 2009. **Evaluation of heat treatment schedules for emerald ash borer (Coleoptera: Buprestidae).** Journal of Economic Entomology. 102: 2048-2055.

U.S. Department of Agriculture, Animal and Plant Health Inspection Service (USDA APHIS). 2011a. **Notice of decision to revise a heat treatment schedule for emerald ash borer.** Federal Register (19 January 2011). 76(12): 3077-3079.

U.S. Department of Agriculture, Animal and Plant Health Inspection Service (USDA APHIS). 2011b. **Risk assessment for the movement of domestic wood packaging material within the United States.** Available at http://www.aphis.usda.gov/plant_health/plant_pest_info/downloads/RiskAssessment-WPM.pdf. [Date accessed unknown].

Zahid, M.I.; Grgurinovic, C.A.; Walsh, D.J. 2008. **Quarantine risks associated with solid wood packaging materials receiving ISPM 15 treatments.** Australian Forestry. 71: 287-293.

THE BEAN PLATASPID, *MEGACOPTA CRIBRARIA*, FEEDING ON KUDZU: AN ACCIDENTAL INTRODUCTION WITH BENEFICIAL EFFECTS

Jim Hanula[1], Yanzhuo Zhang[2], and Scott Horn[1]

[1]U.S. Forest Service, Southern Research Station, Athens, GA 30602
[2]University of Georgia, Department of Entomology, Athens, GA 30602

ABSTRACT

Kudzu, *Pueraria montana* Lour. (Merr.) var. *lobata* (Willd.), is a major weed pest in the southeastern United States where it occupies an estimated 3 million ha (Blaustein 2001) and is spreading at an estimated 50,000 ha per year (Mitich 2000). The bean plataspid, *Megacopta cribraria* (F.), was recently discovered in the United States near Atlanta, GA feeding on kudzu (Suiter et al. 2010). We studied its biology on kudzu and its impact on kudzu growth. We also tested its ability to utilize other common forest legumes for oviposition and development (Zhang et al. 2012)

Flight intercept traps operated from May 17, 2010 to May 31, 2011 in a kudzu field near Athens, GA showed three peaks of adult flight activity, suggesting there are two generations of *M. cribraria* per year on kudzu. Vine samples examined for eggs from April 2010 through April 2011 and June to October 2011 showed two periods of oviposition activity in 2010 which coincided with the peaks in adult activity. In 2011, the second period of oviposition began on or before June 24 and then egg abundance declined gradually thereafter until late August when we recovered <2 eggs/0.5 m of vine. Samples of the five nymphal instars and adults on vines did not show similar trends in abundance. Adults did not lay eggs on the various legume species tested in 2010 in a no-choice test possibly because the cages were too small. In host range experiments conducted in 2011 in kudzu fields using 12 legume species, *M. cribraria* preferentially oviposited on kudzu over soybean, *Glycine max* Merrill., but they still laid 320 eggs/plant on soybean. *Lespedeza hirta* (L.) Hornem. and *Lespedeza cuneata* (Dum. Cours.) G. Don had 122.2 and 108.4 eggs/plant, respectively. Kudzu and soybean were the only species *M. cribraria* completed development on. Plots protected from *M. cribraria* feeding by biweekly insecticide applications had 32.8 percent more kudzu biomass than unprotected plots. Our results show that *M. cribraria* has a significant impact on kudzu growth and could help suppress this pest weed.

The bean plataspid is unique in that it provides beneficial effects by reducing growth of kudzu, but it also has detrimental effects on soybeans where it causes significant yield losses (P. Roberts, pers. comm.). Using data from Grebner et al. (2011) and applying a 6 percent discount rate (D. Grebner, pers. comm.), we estimated that the annual value lost from an acre of land occupied by kudzu was $84/yr, assuming it was an old kudzu infestation that had to be treated from the ground (most expensive eradication procedure). Furthermore, assuming there are 7 million acres of kudzu, the annual potential revenue from those acres is $588 million/yr if pines were growing on them instead of kudzu. In contrast, soybeans were planted on 9 million acres in 2011 in eight southern states (USDA NASS 2011) where kudzu is most prevalent. Assuming a cost of $12/acre to spray for the bean plataspid, the annual cost to spray every acre is $108 million. What these figures do not capture is the ecological cost of kudzu or the cost to soybean growers from having kudzu serve as a reservoir for soybean rust, *Phakopsora pachyrhizi* Syd. & P. Syd. We suggest a balanced approach toward the management of *M. cribraria* and, in particular, the introduction of natural enemies of this insect. The big question that needs to be answered remains, "Is kudzu a necessary part of the cycle that allows this insect to be a pest of soybeans?" If not, then aggressive action should be taken to protect the nearly 80 million acres of soybeans in the United States. However, if kudzu is essential then a more cautious approach is needed that takes into consideration the economic and ecological cost of kudzu's spread across the southern states as well as *M. cribraria*'s impact on soybean production.

Literature Cited

Blaustein, R.J. 2001. **Kudzu's invasion in southern United States life and culture.** In: McNeeley, J.A., ed. The great reshuffling: human dimensions of invasive species. Gland, Switzerland; Cambridge, UK: IUCN: 52-62.

Grebner, D.L.; Ezell, A.W.; Prevost, J.D.; Gaddis, D.A. 2011. **Kudzu control and impact on monetary returns to non-industrial private forest landowners in Mississippi.** Journal of Sustainable Forestry. 30: 204-223.

Mitich, L.W. 2000. **Intriguing world of weeds. Kudzu (*Pueraria lobata* (Willd.) Ohwi.).** Weed Technology. 14: 231-235.

Suiter, D.R.; Eger, J.E., Jr.; Gardner, W.A.; Kemerait, R.C.; All, J.N.; Roberts, P.M.; Greene, J.K.; Ames, L.M.; Buntin, G.D.; Jenkins, T.M.; Douce, G.K. 2010. **Discovery and distribution of *Megacopta cribraria* (Hemiptera: Heteroptera: Plataspidae) in northeast Georgia.** Journal of Integrated Pest Management. 1: 1-4.

U.S. Department of Agriculture, National Agricultural Statistics Service (USDA NASS). 2011. **Acreage.** Available at www.nass.usda.gov/. [Date accessed unknown].

Zhang, Y.; Hanula, J.L.; Horn, S. 2012. **The biology and preliminary host range of *Megacopta cribraria* (F.) (Heteroptera: Plataspidae) and its impact on kudzu growth.** Environmental Entomology: 41(1): 40-50.

PROGRESS IN BIOLOGICAL CONTROL OF MILE-A-MINUTE WEED, *PERSICARIA PERFOLIATA*

Judith A. Hough-Goldstein

University of Delaware, Department of Entomology & Wildlife Ecology, Newark, DE 19716-2160

ABSTRACT

Mile-a-minute weed, *Persicaria perfoliata* (L.) H. Gross, is an invasive annual vine of Asian origin, accidentally introduced near York, PA in the 1930s. It is currently found at sites from Connecticut to North Carolina and west into Ohio, and it continues to spread. A biological control program was initiated in 1996 by the U.S. Forest Service. In 2004, the weevil *Rhinoncomimus latipes* Korotyaev was approved for release in North America. The New Jersey Department of Agriculture Phillip Alampi Beneficial Insect Laboratory has been rearing *R. latipes* since 2004, and in 2011 more than 83,000 weevils were reared and sent to 11 states for release.

With three to four overlapping generations during the growing season, *R. latipes* has the potential for explosive population growth. Weevil outbreaks with severe impacts on mile-a-minute plants have been observed at some, but not all, release sites. To date, the greatest impacts have been observed at sunny sites under warm, dry spring and summer weather conditions where mile-a-minute is in a near-monoculture, but with other competitive plants present. Weevil feeding causes the release of apical dominance and presence of "stacked" nodes resulting in shorter vines which reduce the plant's ability to compete with the resident plant community. Mile-a-minute suppression by *R. latipes* may result in a more diverse mostly native plant community, but where other invasive nonnative plants are present, an "invasive species treadmill" may occur where one invasive species is replaced by another.

Two different experiments were conducted to assess the potential for restoration planting to both enhance plant competition, increasing the effectiveness of the weevils in suppressing mile-a-minute weed, and to help prevent the invasive species treadmill. In the first experiment, conducted by graduate student Ellen Lake, a single application of a pre-emergent herbicide along with revegetation and weevils suppressed mile-a-minute weed and prevented takeover by Japanese stiltgrass (*Microstegium vimineum* [Trin.] A. Camus) where it was present. In the second experiment, conducted by graduate student Kiri Cutting, the greatest suppression of mile-a-minute weed occurred with use of a native seed mix and weevils, compared with no-weevil (insecticide treated) or no-seed treatments. In both experiments, integrated weed management techniques were shown to improve biological control outcomes.

POTENTIAL ECONOMIC IMPACT OF AN
ASIAN LONGHORNED BEETLE OUTBREAK
ON THE NORTHEASTERN FORESTS

Michael Jacobson, Charles Canham, Richard Ready, and Zachary Miller

The Pennsylvania State University, School of Forest Resources, University Park, PA 16802

ABSTRACT

Asian longhorned beetle (ALB), *Anoplophora glabripennis,* is a beetle native to Asia, and like many other invasive species is believed to have been introduced in the United States by wood packaging materials. Unlike other exotic tree borer outbreaks, ALB has numerous hardwood host trees resulting in a potential devastating outcome for the northeastern forests. Of the 50 most common tree species in the northeast, 45 percent are considered preferred and occasional host trees. Asian longhorned beetle was first reported in the United States in New York, NY in 1996. Currently, there have been numerous confirmed outbreaks from Chicago, IL to Boston, MA, primarily near ship port areas. There has been measurable success containing the ALB outbreaks, but the beetle has only been spotted in developed areas and not near large tracts of contiguous forest. This project models annual changes in the forest structure and forest dynamics due to timber harvests, climate change, and volume killed by ALB. The model was created using data from the U.S. Forest Service Forest Inventory Analysis (FIA) reports. The study area included 17 states from Wisconsin to Maine and as far south as Virginia. States that are more susceptible to the ALB outbreak have higher volumes of red maple (*Acer rubrum* L.) and sugar maple (*Acer saccharum* Marsh.). Based on estimated volumes, red and sugar maple made up 84 percent of the total volume killed by ALB over the 100 year period. Between the years 15 and 33 in the model, more tree volume was killed by ALB than was harvested. In present value terms, the difference in harvested value with ALB and without ALB is approximately $16 billion over 100 years. The future outlook of a widespread outbreak would be devastating to the forest products industry, especially those that rely heavily on maple as a primary species. Also, impacts will be more severe in communities that have a higher population of workers in the forest products industry, considering the inevitable market shifts due to an ALB outbreak.

THE TRADE OF PLANTS FOR PLANTING:
AN IMPORTANT PATHWAY OF
INTRODUCTION OF TREE PESTS IN EUROPE

Marc Kenis and René Eschen

CABI Europe-Switzerland, 2800 Delémont, Switzerland

ABSTRACT

Invasive alien pests represent an increasing threat for forest ecosystems and forest biodiversity as well as for forestry production worldwide. The most efficient strategy against invasive species is to mitigate the risk of entry through the management of pathways of introduction. Currently, the importation of woody plants for planting is a key pathway of introduction of tree pests in Europe and elsewhere. Many of the forest pests that have recently invaded Europe were introduced with live plants. Recent examples include the citrus longhorn beetle (*Anoplophora chinensis*), the box tree caterpillar (*Cydalima perspectalis*), the chestnut gall wasp (*Dryocosmus kuriphilus*), and various palm and eucalyptus pests. The live plant trade is also responsible for the movement of dangerous exotic tree pathogens such as *Phythophtora* spp.

Compared to other countries and continents, Europe is relatively permissive regarding the importation of live plants. The European legislation is based on a "black list" system in which only a list of restricted plant species and genera that potentially carry quarantine organisms are forbidden for importation. Pest risk analysis procedures are still largely based on individual pests rather than on pathways or commodities, although it is well known that newly invasive harmful organisms are often unknown or not considered as serious pests before their introduction. Inspection procedures at ports of entry are largely insufficient to prevent the introduction of new organisms, and the increase in the number of inspectors does not follow the increase in importations. Furthermore, there is very little awareness among the public and professionals in Europe compared to other continents, probably because, historically, Europe has suffered less from invasive plant pests and pathogens than other continents.

In order to propose and establish efficient and generic measures for mitigation against invading forest pests along the plants for planting pathway in Europe, there is a need to better understand this pathway and all its components. In the framework of the EU COST (European Cooperation In Science and Technology) Action PERMIT (Pathway Evaluation and pest Risk Management In Transport) and the EU FP7 project ISEFOR (Increasing Sustainability of European Forests), we are presently assessing the importance of the trade of woody plants for planting in the invasion of alien tree pests in Europe through analyses of plant pest interception data from national and regional plant protection organisations, as well as data on the establishment of alien pests. These analyses confirm that, in Europe, the live plant trade is by far the main pathway of introduction of pests and pathogens of woody plants, and that introductions of plant pests and pathogens though this pathway have increased in recent years. They also show that, while the majority of interceptions are made on plants imported from Asia, many recently established pests and pathogens of woody plants still come from North America. Introductions from South America, Oceania, and Africa are also increasing.

In these two projects, we are using cases of alien tree pests known or strongly suspected of having been recently introduced with woody plants for planting to identify further weaknesses in the present systems of management and phytosanitary measures in Europe. We are also carrying out a global review to identify best practices elsewhere.

Some of the recommendations for a more efficient management of the plant for planting pathway of introduction into Europe include: (1) moving from species-based pests risk analyses to commodity-based pest risk analysis (i.e., moving from the "quarantine organism" concept to the assumption that every poorly-known exotic herbivorous arthropod or plant pathogen may represent a danger for plant health when moved to another continent); (2) developing new systems approaches including new methods, such as the establishment of sentinel nurseries in the exporting regions; (3) rapid implementation of International Standard for Phytosanitation Measures (ISPM) for plants for planting presently developed by the International Plant Protection Convention (IPPC); (4) strengthening legislation regarding soil importation and size of imported plants; (5) increasing phytosanitary inspection capacities; and (6) increasing awareness among the public and professionals, for example, to provide incentives to produce locally and buy plants grown locally.

OVERVIEW OF THE U.S. ASIAN LONGHORNED BEETLE (ALB) ERADICATION EFFORT

Phillip A. Lewis

[1]USDA APHIS, PPQ, CPHST, Buzzards Bay, MA 02542

ABSTRACT

The Asian Longhorned Beetle (ALB) Eradication Program has applied a systemic insecticide (imidacloprid) to tens of thousands of trees as part of their area-wide eradication and control strategy. Host trees are treated when located within close proximity of trees that have been removed due to an active ALB infestation. The treatments target the adult beetles as they feed on twigs and leaves and have shown consistent effectiveness in numerous field trials in China. In New York, the majority of treatments is via soil injection and is directed below ground and close to the base of the tree. Uptake of the pesticide into the root system and growing portions of the tree is slow, taking several months before peak levels are achieved. A second tree treatment method used by the Program, mainly in Massachusetts, is a direct trunk application of an injectable imidacloprid formulation. Small drill holes are made in the trunk of the tree at the base and a small amount (4 mL) of product per hole is forced under pressure into the tree's vascular system. Uptake by the tree using this system is very rapid, with high levels of pesticide observed after only 1 or 2 weeks. Chemical applications are accomplished in the spring and early summer, targeting latent populations of the adult beetles that begin emerging from infested trees in late June to early July.

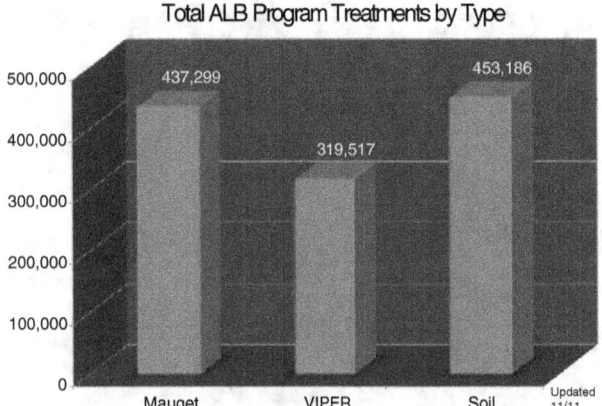

Figure 1.—Number of tree treatments, by type, 2000 to 2011.

Treatment effectiveness. In 2010, the ALB Eradication Program reached a milestone of 1 million tree treatments (Fig 1). This total represents close to 400,000 trees having received the desired 3 consecutive years of treatment. In addition to chemical treatments of at-risk trees, the Program's comprehensive approach includes public awareness campaigns, industry education, infested tree removals, and extensive tree survey. This multi-level attack on ALB populations has led to successful eradications in Chicago, IL, Jersey City, NJ, and Islip, NY. Additional eradication declarations are anticipated over the next few years as New Jersey has not had ALB detected since 2006, and in New York, ALB has not been found in Manhattan since 2005 (Fig 2).

There are a number of metrics that can be considered when determining the efficacy of the chemical treatments, the foremost being that there has not been a single known case of adult emergence from a tree that has received the full 3 consecutive years of chemical treatment. Other indicators are the steady decline in the number of infested trees found at each of the infestation locations, as displayed in Figure 3. ALB infestations in NY, NJ, and IL have seen rapid and consistent declines in the number of infested trees due to overall program activities and outreach efforts. The infestation in Worcester shows a similar trend, although

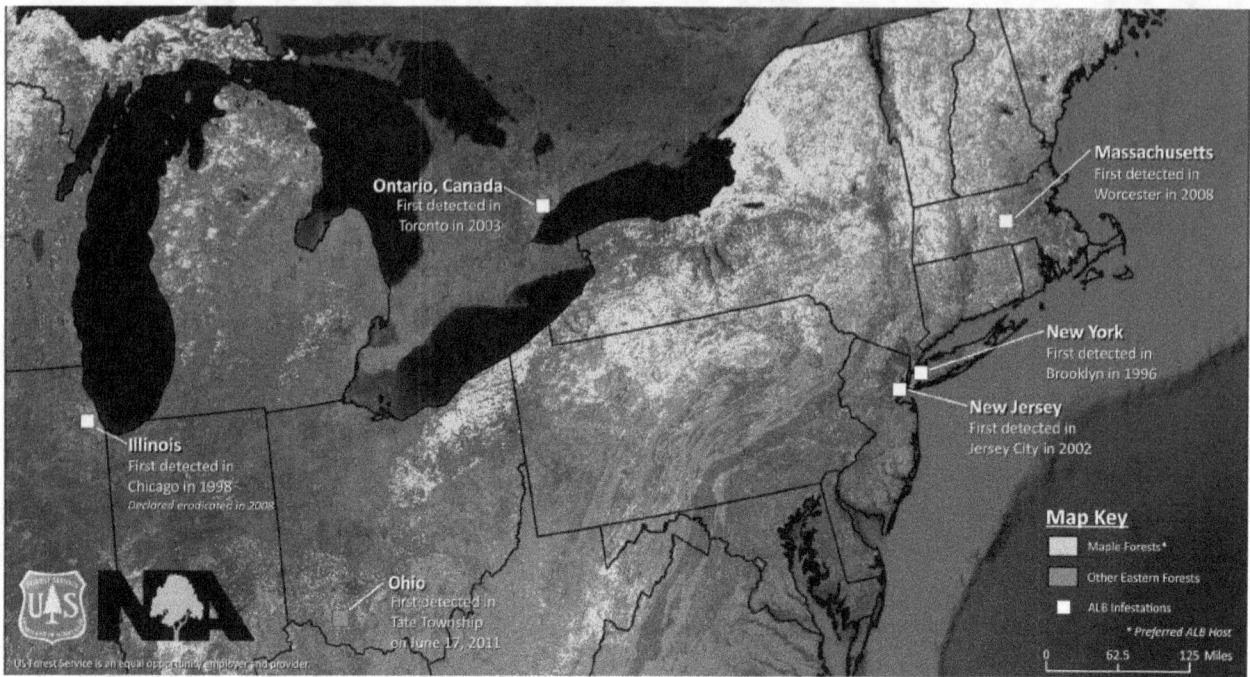

Figure 2.—Map of North American ALB infestations.

the number of infested trees after 3 ½ years of activity is just now at the point of the peak of the NY infestation in 1999 (Fig. 4). The Ohio infestation currently stands at more than 5,000 trees, but delimitation surveys are just beginning. The latter two infestations pose clear challenges to the treatment program due to their size and unchecked spread of the beetles for many years. Changes to treatment and survey activities may be necessary to contain and eliminate these extensive ALB populations.

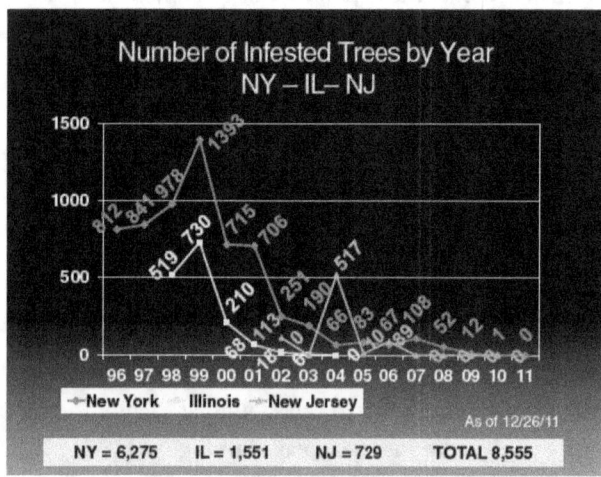

Figure 3.—Number of infested trees over time by location.

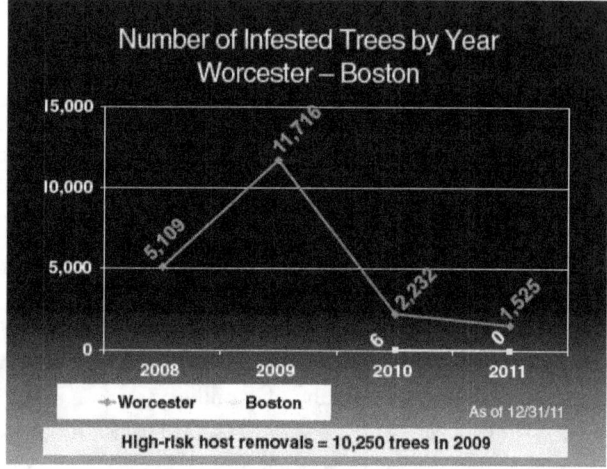

Figure 4.—Number of infested trees by year in Worcester and Boston.

AN OVERVIEW OF CERAMBYCID BEETLE
PHEROMONE CHEMISTRY

Jocelyn G. Millar[1] and Lawrence M. Hanks[2]

[1]University of California, Department of Entomology, Riverside, CA 92521
[2]University of Illinois at Urbana-Champaign, Department of Entomology, Urbana, IL 61801

ABSTRACT

The family Cerambycidae comprises more than 30,000 described species. Much of their biology is still relatively unknown, in part because of their long life cycles, making them difficult to study. In their native ranges, some species are significant pests of forest, orchard, and ornamental trees, as well as damaging to saw logs, lumber, and wooden structures. Many species have the potential to be invasive because the larvae can be readily moved to new countries in pallets, dunnage, furniture, and other wooden objects. Examples of several recent invaders include Asian longhorned beetle (*Anoplophora glabripennis*), eucalyptus borers (*Phoracantha* spp.), and the Japanese small cedar borer (*Callidiellum rufipenne* [Motschulsky]). Other potentially invasive species have been detected in small numbers at ports of entry.

Pheromone-baited traps are widely used as tools for detection and sampling of both native and exotic pests. However, despite their economic importance and potential invasiveness, until recently almost nothing was known about pheromone use by cerambycids. The general consensus was that cerambycids were unlikely to use pheromones for long distance attraction to any great extent. For example, a 2004 review (Allison et al. 2004) listed pheromones for fewer than 10 species, all of which appeared to be only weakly attractive, and none of which were developed for practical applications. Instead of using pheromones, cerambycids were thought to rely on a strong attraction to their host plants, for which there was some supporting evidence.

In 2004 we took a second look at pheromone use by cerambycids because volatile pheromones are so widespread amongst other insect groups, and it seemed unlikely that cerambycids would have abandoned such a successful method of signaling between conspecifics. We identified three broad objectives:

1. To determine the importance of pheromones in cerambycid beetle biology and their functional roles including which species produce pheromones, what they are used for and in what context, and if there are behaviors and morphologies diagnostic for pheromone use.

2. To develop an overall picture of the pheromone chemistry, including the types of compounds used and differences and similarities between pheromones of related species.

3. To develop the ability to predict whether a particular species will use pheromones, and the likely pheromone structures, based on the beetle's taxonomic placement. Such predictions would greatly accelerate the process of identifying pheromones for new invaders.

Thus, we hoped to develop a better understanding of cerambycid semiochemistry and to use that knowledge to develop tools for detection and management of both native and exotic pest species.

We took two approaches. First, we synthesized a library of all known cerambycid pheromones and a number of analogs and homologs and tested them in field bioassays. Second, to fill in gaps in our knowledge of pheromone use within the taxonomic subgroups, we targeted species in tribes and subfamilies in which no pheromones were known. As new pheromones were identified, they were incorporated into the screening library. Both approaches were extremely successful. From the screening trials, we have identified likely pheromones for several hundred cerambycid species, and the number is increasing every year. This has included a number of invasive species, such as *Monochamus alternatus* (Teale et al. 2011) and *Monochamus sutor*, and we have strong leads on pheromones of other important invasive species, such as *Anaplophora chinensis*. With support from the U.S. Department of Agriculture Animal and Plant Health Inspection Service (USDA APHIS), we have expanded our screening trials all across the United States and into China, Australia, New Zealand, South America, Europe, and most recently, southern Africa.

We also identified pheromones of species in new cerambycid tribes and subfamilies where previously no pheromones were known. Thus, we identified 3,5-dimethyldodecanoic acid (Fig. 1) from *Prionus californicus*, the first pheromone for a cerambycid in the subfamily Prioninae (Rodstein et al. 2009). This was important for several reasons. First, this was the first example of a female-produced pheromone within the Cerambycidae, showing that females as well as males used long-range pheromones. Second, the pheromone attracted males from hundreds of meters away, dispelling the notion that long-distance pheromones were not important for cerambycids. Third, this pheromone was highly conserved within the genus; it is the sex pheromone of at least 12 North American as well as the 1 European *Prionus* species (Barbour et al. 2011). We have also identified a different female

sex pheromone for species in the prionine genus *Tragosoma* (Ray et al. submitted), and Matthew Ginzel at Purdue University is working on the identification of a pheromone for the prionine *Mallodon dasystomus*. Furthermore, we have identified the first long-range pheromones from the subfamily Lepturinae. Female *Ortholeptura valida* produce *cis*-vaccenyl acetate (Fig. 1) (Ray et al. 2011), whereas female *Desmocerus californicus californicus* produce desmolactone (Fig. 1) (Ray et al. 2012). Currently, it is unclear whether these structures will prove to be attractive to congeners.

In tandem with our work, there has been a strong revival of interest in identifying and exploiting cerambycid pheromones, as described by other presenters in this forum. For example, John Sweeney and Peter Silk in Canada identified fuscumol and fuscumol acetate (Fig. 1) from *Tetropium* spp., and in screening trials similar to ours, showed that these and other known pheromones attracted numerous species across Canada and in Europe and China (Silk et al. 2007, Sweeney et al. 2010). Paulo Zarbin identified fuscumol and fuscumol acetate as pheromones for a Brazilian species. We have since shown that fuscumol

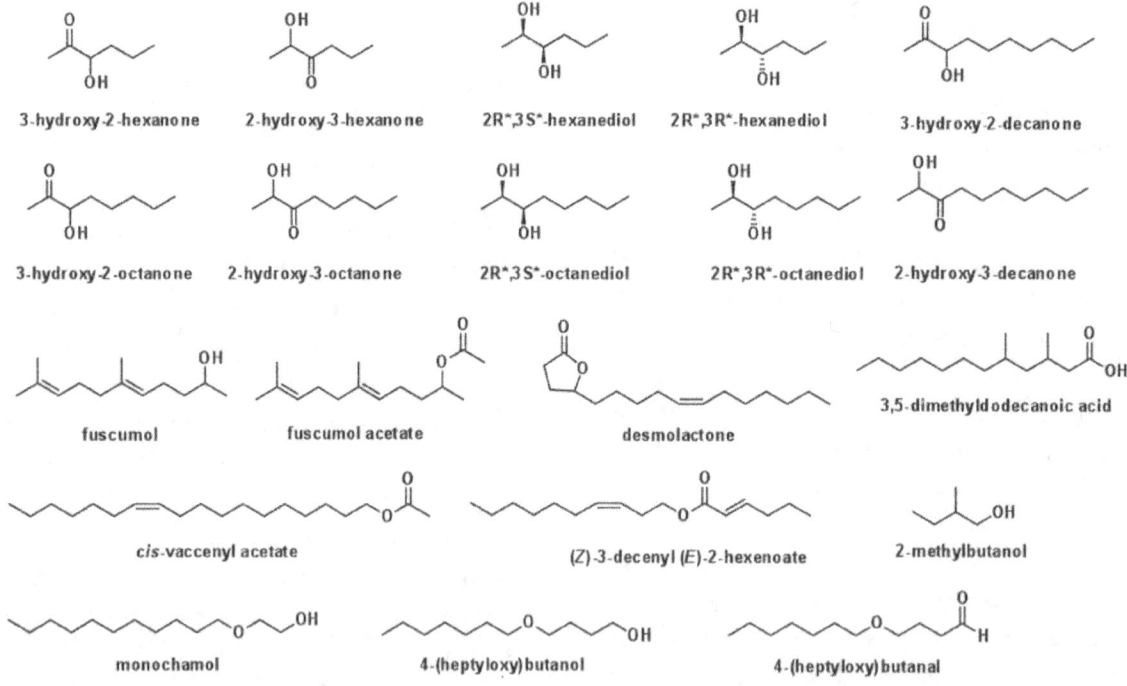

Figure 1.—Structures of known volatile sex or aggregation pheromones from cerambycid beetles.

and fuscumol acetate are likely pheromones for other lamiines in North America and Asia (Mitchell et al. 2011).

David Hall and Juan Pajares identified monochamol (Fig. 1) as the pheromone of *Monochamus galloprovincialis* (Pajares et al. 2010). This catalyzed our identification of pheromones for a cascade of *Monochamus* spp. in Asia and North America, including *M. alternatus*, *M. scutellatus*, *M. notatus*, *M. carolinensis*, *M. clamator*, *M. obtusus*, and *M. tillator*.

A number of trends are emerging from this explosion of recent work on cerambycid pheromones:

- It is clear that long-range pheromones are widely used amongst the Cerambycidae, and they can be very powerful, attracting beetles from hundreds of meters away.

- There is often pheromone parsimony, with the same or similar compounds being used as pheromones by a number of species. For example, 3-hydroxy-2-hexanone is the pheromone of numerous cerambycine species, whereas fuscumol and fuscumol acetate are broadly attractive to species in the subfamilies Lamiinae and Spondylidinae. This is useful for practical purposes because one compound can be used to attract multiple species.

- Male-produced pheromones are produced in large amounts (>0.1 mg per beetle per hour). Consequently, lures for these species must release pheromone at rates of several mg per day.

- For the subfamilies Cerambycinae, Lamiinae, and Spondylidinae, attractant pheromones are produced by males, whereas females produce pheromones in the Prioninae and Lepturinae.

- Trap design is critical, and to be most effective, traps should be coated with liquid Teflon®, which can improve trap captures by more than an order of magnitude (Graham et al. 2010).

Since 2004, we have worked with collaborators across the United States and overseas to develop an overview of how broadly attractive these pheromones might be. The results have exceeded our expectations, with hundreds of species being attracted. Some highlights of this work include:

- Since 2009, collaborator Sven-Eric Spichiger (Pennsylvania Department of Agriculture, in collaboration with USDA Cooperative Agricultural Pest Survey) has caught more than 16,000 beetles in 135 species, using subsets of pheromone library.

- In the past 2 years, collaborators Elizabeth Graham, Therese Poland, and Deborah McCullough have screened subsets of our library of compounds in Michigan, catching a large number of species.

- In 2010-11, U.S. and Canadian collaborators trapped a number of *Monochamus* species with our screening library (e.g., Macias-Samano et al. 2012).

- Field trials in China have resulted in the identification of the pheromone of Monochamus alternatus and leads towards identification of *Anoplophora chinensis* and *Monochamus sutor* from the USDA APHIS list of the 13 most dangerous Asian species.

So what remains to be done to translate this work from the research to the operational level? There are several important issues that need to be resolved. First, as a step towards commercialization of pheromone lures, in 2011 we tested lures prepared by two companies (Synergy and Chemtica), and lures from both companies performed as well or better than our homemade lures. Furthermore, the commercial lures had field lifetimes of at least several weeks.

Second, we have tested the concept of preparing generic pheromone lures that contain a mixture of pheromones for attracting a number of species simultaneously. In general, this idea has worked well, with only a few cases of one species being inhibited by the pheromone of another. If these types of generic lures can be used, it will cut down on the number of monitoring traps that are needed for surveillance programs.

Third, we need to develop a better understanding of the role of host plant volatiles in combination with the pheromones. From preliminary trials in 2011 and from results from other groups, it is clear that many cerambycid species are optimally attracted by combinations of pheromones with host volatiles. Some species are not attracted to either pheromone alone or host volatiles alone, whereas combining the two increases trap captures by one to two orders of magnitude. Working out the details of the interaction of pheromones and host volatiles will be one of our major foci for the next couple of years.

In summary, we have learned a tremendous amount about cerambycid pheromones in a short time, and this whole research area has changed from a little-known and poorly studied field to one which is seeing exponential growth in interest, awareness, and potential. Contrary to the general view of only a few years ago that pheromones played only a minor role in cerambycid biology, it has become clear that volatile pheromones are widely used throughout the family. This in turn has opened up new opportunities for the exploitation of these pheromones for detection, sampling, and management of these beetles.

Acknowledgments

We thank Victor Mastro (USDA APHIS), the Alphawood Foundation, and the USDA Cooperative State Research, Education, and Extension Service (CSREES) for grants in support of this work. We also thank our numerous collaborators for their assistance, including Sven-Eric Spichiger, Therese Poland, Deborah McCullough, Elizabeth Graham, Steve Teale, Jeremy Allison, Melissa Fierke, and Jacob Wickham, amongst many others.

Literature Cited

Allison, J.D.; Borden, J.H.; Seybold, S.J. 2004. **A review of the chemical ecology of the Cerambycidae (Coleoptera).** Chemoecology. 14: 123-150.

Barbour, J.D; Millar, J.G.; Rodstein, J.; Ray, A.M.; Alston, D.G.; Rejzek, M.; Dutcher, J.D.; Hanks; L.M. 2011. **Synthetic 3,5-dimethyldodecanoic acid serves as a general attractant for multiple species of *Prionus* (Coleoptera: Cerambycidae).** Annals of the Entomological Society of America. 104: 588-593.

Graham, E.E.; Mitchell, R.F.; Reagel, P.F.; Barbour, J.D.; Millar, J.G.; Hanks, L.M. 2010. **Treating panel traps with a fluoropolymer dramatically enhances their efficiency in capturing cerambycid beetles.** Journal of Economic Entomology. 103: 641-647.

Macias-Samano, J.E.; Wakerchuk, D.; Millar, J.G.; Hanks. L.M. [In press]. **2-Undecyloxy-1-ethanol in combination with other semiochemicals attracts three *Monochamus* species (Coleoptera: Cerambycidae) in British Columbia.** Canadian Entomologist.

Mitchell, R.F.; Graham, E.E.; Wong, J.C.H.; Reagel, P.F.; Striman, B.L.; Hughes, G.P.; Paschen, M.A.; Ginzel, M.D.; Millar, J.G.; Hanks, L.M. 2011. **Fuscumol and fuscumol acetate are general attractants for many species of cerambycid beetles in the subfamily Lamiinae.** Entomologia Experimentalis et Applicata.141: 71-77.

Pajares, J.A.; Alvarez, G.; Ibeas, F.; Gallego, D.; Hall, D.R.; Farman, D. I. 2010. **Identification and field activity of a male-produced aggregation pheromone in the pine sawyer beetle, *Monochamus galloprovincialis*.** Journal of Chemical Ecology. 36: 570–583.

Ray, A.M.; Žunič, A.; Alten, R.L.; McElfresh, J.S.; Hanks, L.M.; Millar. J.G. 2011. **cis-Vaccenyl acetate, a sex attractant pheromone of *Ortholeptura valida*, a longhorned beetle in the subfamily Lepturinae.** Journal of Chemical Ecology. 37: 173-178.

Rodstein, J.; McElfresh, J.S.; Barbour, J.D.; Ray, A.M.; Hanks, L.M.; Millar, J.G. 2009. **Identification and synthesis of a female-produced sex pheromone for the cerambycid beetle *Prionus californicus*.** Journal of Chemical Ecology. 35: 590-600.

Silk, P.J.; Sweeney, J.; Wu, J.; Price, J.; Gutowski, J.M.; Kettela, E.G. 2007. **Evidence for a male-produced pheromone in *Tetropium fuscum* (F.) and *Tetropium cinnamopterum* (Kirby) (Coleoptera: Cerambycidae).** Naturwissenschaften. 94: 697–701.

Sweeney, J.; Silk, P.J.; Gutowski, J.M.; Wu, J.; Lemay, M.A.; Mayo, P.D.; Magee, D.I. 2010. **Effect of chirality, release rate, and host volatiles on response of *Tetropium fuscum* (F.), *Tetropium cinnamopterum* Kirby, and *Tetropium castaneum* (L.) to the aggregation pheromone, fuscumol.** Journal of Chemical Ecology. 36(12): 1309-1321.

Teale, S.A.; Wickham, J.D.; Zhang, F.; Su, J.; Chen, Y.; Xiao, W.; Hanks, L.M.; Millar, J.G. 2011. **A male-produced aggregation pheromone of *Monochamus alternatus* (Coleoptera: Cerambycidae), a major vector of pine wood nematode.** Journal of Economic Entomology. 104: 1592-1598.

TRAPPING PINE CERAMBYCIDS

Daniel R. Miller

U.S. Forest Service, Southern Research Station, Athens, GA 30602

ABSTRACT

Our goal was to develop a robust trapping system for bark and wood boring beetles and their associates in pine stands of North America. For Cerambycidae, we focused on the southern pine sawyer, *Monochamus titillator* (F.), due to its abundance and pest status in damaging lumber and vectoring pine wood nematodes, a causal agent of pine wilt disease. Research trials were conducted with numerous collaborators representing State and Private Forestry, National Forests and Research Stations (U.S. Forest Service), four Forestry Centers with the Canadian Forest Service, six universities, and several provincial and state agencies. My presentation dealt with the following five issues: 1) use of wet vs. dry cup with funnel traps; 2) attractant kairomone blends for cerambycids; 3) funnel or panel trap type ; 4) lure position in funnel traps (inside vs. outside); and 5) a modified funnel trap. Solutions used in wet cup trapping include RV and marine antifreeze and solutions of propylene glycol or salt. The benefits of using wet cups over dry cups with an insecticide strip are: 1) lower levels of damage to beetles; and 2) increased retention of captured cerambycids.

We focused on host kairomones as attractants to broadly sample the guild of bark and wood boring beetles. Two common host compounds, ethanol and α-pinene, were mildly attractive to *M. titillator* in the southeastern United States (Miller 2006). In testing the bark beetle pheromones ipsenol, ipsdienol, and lanierone, we found that *M. titillator* was strongly attracted to funnel traps baited with ipsenol and ipsdienol (Miller and Asaro 2005). Larval *M. titillator* are facultative predators on bark beetles. In 2006, we tested the quaternary blend of ethanol, α-pinene, ipsenol, and ipsdienol (Q lure) against the binary combinations of ethanol plus α-pinene and ipsenol plus ipsdienol in Louisiana, Georgia, Florida, and Virginia. Funnel traps baited with the Q lure outperformed those baited with either binary

blend in catching *M. titillator* at all locations (Miller et al. 2011). In addition, we found that *Monochamus scutellatus* (Say) was attracted to traps baited with the Q lure in Virginia.

Previously in Canada, kairomone studies combining host volatiles with bark beetle pheromones were found to be effective at attracting several species of *Monochamus* (Allison et al. 2001, de Groot and Nott 2004). With the aid of numerous collaborators, we tested the Q lure and both binary blends at 22 locations across Canada and the USA. In addition to *M. titillator*, traps baited with the Q lure were consistently attractive to *M. scutellatus*, *Monochamus carolinensis* (Olivier), *Monochamus mutator* LeConte, *Monochamus clamator* (LeConte), *Monochamus notatus* (Drury), and *M. obtusus* Casey as well as some other species of Cerambycidae. Five groups of responders were noted in the study. Group 1 included species attracted to the Q lure, including seven species of *Monochamus* as well as other common cerambycids such as *Acanthocinus obsoletus* (Olivier), *Acanthocinus princeps* (Walker), *Astylopsis arcuata* (LeConte), *Astylopsis sexguttata* (Say), and *Rhagium inquisitor* (L.). Group 2 consisted of species such as *Acmaeops proteus* (Kirby), *Arhopalus asperatus* (LeConte), *Asemum striatum* (L.), *Megasemum aspersum* (LeConte), *Xestoleptura crassicornis* (LeConte), and *Xylotrechus longitarsis* Casey that were attracted to the binary combination of ethanol and α-pinene and unaffected by the presence of ipsenol and ipsdienol. Group 3 included *Acanthocinus obliquus* (LeConte) and *M. scutellatus* that, when in stands of spruce, were attracted to the binary combination of ipsenol and ipsdienol but were unaffected by the presence of ethanol and α-pinene. Group 4 included one common species, *Neospondylis upiformis* (Mannerheim), that was attracted to traps baited with ethanol and α-pinene and was interrupted by the presence of ipsenol and ipsdienol.

Group 5 consisted of numerous species caught in low numbers with no clear treatment preferences (singletons).

In comparing multiple-funnel traps to panel traps baited with ethanol and α-pinene, we found that panel traps outperformed funnel traps in capturing *M. titillator* and *Acanthocinus nodosus* (F.) (Miller and Crowe 2011). However, funnel traps were as good as panel traps for *Arhopalus rusticus* (LeConte) and *Xylotrechus sagittatus* (Germar). One issue with funnel traps is the placement of lures which must be outside the funnel since they are too big to fit inside the funnels. Lindgren (1983) found that placing lures for ambrosia beetles inside funnels increased catches, likely due to the increased dispersal of odors throughout the trap when lures are placed inside funnels. We modified funnel traps by increasing the hole in each funnel from 5 cm to 12 cm to allow placement of large lures inside funnels. Catches of *M. titillator, A. nodosus, A. obsoletus, X. sagittatus,* and *A. sexguttata* in modified funnel traps with lures placed inside the funnels were twice those in regular funnel traps (all baited with Q lure). We compared modified traps with lures placed outside the funnels as well as inside the funnels to panel traps on catches of woodborers (all baited with Q lure). Modified traps with lures placed inside the funnels outperformed panel traps as well as modified traps with lures placed outside the funnels for *M. titillator, A. obsoletus, X. sagittatus,* and *Astylopsis* spp.

In summary, to catch a broad array of pine woodborers and associates use the following: 1) wet cups with solution of propylene glycol or salt; 2) a lure blend consisting of ethanol, α-pinene, ipsenol and ipsdienol; 3) panel and/or modified multiple-funnel traps; and 4) lures placed within the funnels when using multiple-funnel traps.

Literature Cited

Allison, J.D.; Borden, J.H.; McIntosh, R.L.; de Groot, P.; Gries, R. 2001. **Kairomonal response by four *Monochamus* species (Coleoptera: Cerambycidae) to bark beetle pheromones.** Journal of Chemical Ecology. 27: 633-646.

de Groot, P.; Nott, R.W. 2004. **Response of the whitespotted sawyer beetle, *Monochamus s. scutellatus*, and associated woodborers to pheromones of some *Ips* and *Dendroctonus* bark beetles.** Journal of Applied Entomology. 128: 483-487.

Lindgren, B.S. 1983. **A multiple-funnel trap for scolytid beetles (Coleoptera).** Canadian Entomologist. 115: 299-302.

Miller, D.R. 2006. **Ethanol and (-)-α-pinene: attractant kairomones for some large wood-boring beetles in southeastern USA.** Journal of Chemical Ecology. 32: 779-794.

Miller, D.R.; Asaro, C. 2005. **Ipsenol and ipsdienol attract *Monochamus titillator* (Coleoptera: Cerambycidae) and associated large pine woodborers in southeastern United States.** Journal of Economic Entomology. 98: 2033-2040.

Miller, D.R.; Asaro, C.; Crowe, C.M.; Duerr, D.A. 2011. **Bark beetle pheromones and pine volatiles: attractant kairomone lure blend for longhorn beetles (Cerambycidae) in pine stands of the southeastern United States.** Journal of Economic Entomology. 104: 1245-1257.

Miller, D.R.; Crowe, C.M. 2011. **Relative performance of Lindgren multiple-funnel, panel and Colossus pipe traps in catching Cerambycidae and associated species in the southeastern United States.** Journal of Economic Entomology. 104: 1934-1941.

IDENTIFYING MECHANISMS OF RESISTANCE OF HEMLOCK TO THE HEMLOCK WOOLLY ADELGID, *ADELGES TSUGAE* ANNAND (HEMIPTERA: ADELGIDAE)

Kelly L.F. Oten

North Carolina State University, Department of Entomology,
Raleigh, NC 27695

ABSTRACT

The hemlock woolly adelgid (HWA), *Adelges tsugae* Annand (Hemiptera: Adelgidae), is an invasive forest pest that threatens the existence of eastern hemlock (*Tsuga canadensis* (L.) Carr.) and Carolina hemlock (*T. caroliniana* Engelm.) in the eastern United States. Using its elongated stylet bundle to penetrate host parenchyma cells (Young et al. 1995), the insect causes a decline in tree health, manifested by needle drop, bud abortion, inhibition of new growth (McClure 1991), physiological drought-like symptoms (Walker-Lane 2009), and an increased level of hydrogen peroxide (H_2O_2) (Radville et al. 2011). A susceptible hemlock dies in as few as 4 years but may survive beyond 10 years (McClure 1987, 1991). The invasive population in the eastern United States was first detected near Richmond, VA in 1951. The range of HWA in the east has since spread through the range of hemlocks, now affecting 18 states (USDA FS 2011). The mortality caused by HWA to eastern and a Carolina hemlock is tremendous. Approximately 80-90 percent of infested hemlocks native to the eastern United States have already vanished as a result of this exotic insect (Hale 2004, Townsend and Rieske-Kinney 2006). Moreover, the production of hemlocks for the ornamental industry, valued at $34 million between Tennessee and North Carolina alone, has been virtually eliminated.

HWA is native to eastern Asia and Northwestern North America where it is described as a minor pest and is almost never associated with tree mortality (Annand 1924, Bentz et al. 2002, Havill et al. 2006, Keen 1938). The mechanism of resistance and/or tolerance in these hemlock species is unknown. For years, it was believed that eastern and Carolina hemlocks were entirely and exclusively susceptible to HWA. However, in the wake of widespread mortality, anecdotal evidence suggested surviving individuals or stands of eastern and Carolina hemlocks may be less susceptible. This has since been corroborated by research, and distinct populations have been selected and continue to be pursued as putatively resistant to HWA (Caswell et al. 2008, Ingwell and Preisser 2010, Kaur 2009). In addition, Carolina hemlock has been identified as less susceptible to HWA than eastern hemlock (Jetton et al. 2008, Oten 2011).

The purpose of this research was to investigate mechanisms of host-plant resistance of hemlocks to the hemlock woolly adelgid. Understanding this more thoroughly may facilitate or expedite progress towards the development of a resistant hemlock by identifying characteristics that can be used in the selection of individuals within natural stands or to screen within a breeding program.

Surface morphology of six hemlock species and a hybrid was investigated using low-temperature scanning electron microscopy. Observations focused on trichome presence and placement and cuticle thickness. These characteristics were studied in the context of species-level host-plant resistance to HWA. The species observed were: eastern hemlock, Carolina hemlock, western hemlock (*T. heterophylla* [Raf.] Sarg.), mountain hemlock (*T. mertensiana* [Bong.] Carr.), Chinese hemlock (*T. chinensis* [Franch.] E. Pritz.), southern Japanese hemlock (*T. sieboldii* Carr.), northern Japanese hemlock (*T. diversifolia* [Maxim.] Mast.), and a *T. chinensis x caroliniana* hybrid bred by the National Arboretum (Bentz et al. 2002). While trichomes likely do not play a role in resistance to HWA, we found that cuticle thickness may. When comparing cuticle thickness at different locations on the needle pulvinus, the point where HWA consistently insert their stylets is statistically thinner than the other locations measured. This may translate to a lesser obstacle for HWA to overcome for feeding success. In addition, Chinese hemlock, the most resistant hemlock species, had the thickest overall cuticle. At the insertion point only, it was not statistically significant from other resistant species, suggesting that a thicker external cuticle may interrupt host-plant selection processes of HWA when feeding upon Chinese hemlock.

We also assessed the chemical profiles of epicuticular waxes of the different hemlock species using gas chromatography/mass spectrometry. Our results indicated both inter- and intraspecific variation in the compounds present. In addition, a single, unidentified compound was present in all resistant hemlock samples and 1 of the 14 eastern hemlock samples. This research is ongoing.

Finally, we surveyed for the presence of trophically-related enzymes used by HWA. We detected trypsin-like protease, amylase, peroxidase, and polyphenol oxidase. The presence of these enzymes was revealing of the insect's feeding habits, but also suggests possible interactions between HWA and its host. For example, some plants are capable of inducing biochemical pathways that result in the production of enzyme inhibitors. If resistant hemlocks are capable of doing this, it may be the advantage that enables them to lower HWA infestations rate and ultimately survive. Hemlocks should be surveyed for the ability to inhibit these enzymes.

The future of the hemlock in the eastern United States is uncertain. Implementing host-plant resistance into an Integrated Pest Management Program along with biological control and judicious use of chemical control could provide lasting HWA management. To succeed, it is critical that we continue current research to unveil and understand the mechanism(s) of resistance and ultimately develop a hemlock variety resistant to HWA.

Literature Cited

Annand, P.N. 1924. **A new species of *Adelges* (Hemiptera: Phylloxeridae).** Pan-Pacific Entomologist. 1: 79-82.

Bentz, S.E.; Riedel, L.G.H.; Pooler, M.R.; Townsend, A.M. 2002. **Hybridization and self-compatibility in controlled pollinations of eastern North American and Asian hemlock (*Tsuga*) species.** Journal of Arboriculture. 28: 200-205.

Caswell, T.; Casagrande, R.; Maynard, B.; Preisser, E. 2008. **Production and evaluation of eastern hemlocks potentially resistant to the hemlock woolly adelgid.** In: Onken, B.; Rheardon, R., eds. Fourth symposium on the hemlock woolly adelgid in the eastern United States; 12-14 February 2008; Hartford, CT. FHTET-2008-01. Morgantown, WV: U.S. Department of Agriculture, Forest Service, Forest Health Technology Enterprise Team: 124-134.

Hale, F.A. 2004. **The hemlock woolly adelgid: a threat to hemlock in Tennessee.** SP503-G. Knoxville, TN: The University of Tennessee, Agricultural Extension Service. 4 p.

Havill, N.P.; Montgomery, M.E.; Yu, G.; Shiyake, S.; Caccone, A. 2006. **Mitochondrial DNA from hemlock woolly adelgid (Hemiptera: Adelgidae) suggests cryptic speciation and pinpoints the source of the introduction to eastern North America.** Annals of the Entomological Society of America. 99: 195-203.

Ingwell, L.L.; Preisser, E.L. 2010. **Using citizen science programs to identify host resistance in pest-invaded forests.** Conservation Biology. 25: 182-188.

Jetton, R.M.; Hain, F.P; Dvorak, W.S.; Frampton, J. 2008. **Infestation rate of hemlock woolly adelgid (Hemiptera: Adelgidae) among three North American hemlock (*Tsuga*) species following artificial inoculation.** Journal of Entomological Science. 43: 438-442.

Kaur, N. 2009. **Developing artificial rearing techniques for hemlock woolly adelgid, *Adelges tsugae* and balsam woolly adelgid, *Adelges piceae;* artificial infestation and epicuticular wax study of Carolina hemlock, *Tsuga caroliniana,* provenances.** Raleigh, NC: North Carolina State University. M.S. thesis.

Keen, F.P. 1938. **Insect enemies of western forests.** U.S. Department of Agriculture Miscellaneous Publication 273. Washington, DC: Government Printing Office.

McClure, M.S. 1987. **Biology and control of hemlock woolly adelgid.** Bull. 851. New Haven, CT: Connecticut Agricultural Experiment Station.

McClure, M.S. 1991. **Density-dependent feedback and population cycles in *Adelges tsugae* (Homoptera: Adelgidae) on *Tsuga canadensis.*** Environmental Entomology. 20: 258-264.

Oten, K.L.F. 2011. **Host-plant selection by the hemlock woolly adelgid, *Adelges tsugae* Annand: sensory systems and feeding behavior in relation to physical and chemical host-plant characteristics.** Raleigh, NC: North Carolina State University. Ph.D. dissertation.

Radville, L.; Chaves, A.; Preisser, E.L. 2011. **Variation in plant defense against invasive herbivores: evidence for a hypersensitive response in eastern hemlocks (*Tsuga canadensis*).** Journal of Chemical Ecology. 37: 592-597.

Townsend, L.; Rieske-Kinney, L. 2006. **Meeting the threat of the hemlock woolly adelgid.** ENTFACT-452. Somerset, KY: University of Kentucky, Pulaski County Cooperative Extension Service. 4 p.

U.S. Department of Agriculture, Forest Service (USDA FS). 2011. **Counties with established HWA populations 2010**. Available at http://na.fs.fed.us/fhp/hwa/maps/2010.pdf. [Date accessed unknown].

Walker-Lane, L.N. 2009. **The effect of hemlock woolly adelgid infestation on water relations of Carolina and eastern Hemlock.** Raleigh, NC: North Carolina State University. M.S. thesis.

Young, R.F.; Shields, K.S.; Berlyn, G.P. 1995. **Hemlock woolly adelgid (Homoptera: Adelgidae): stylet bundle insertion and feeding sites.** Annals of the Entomological Society of America. 88: 827-835.

DETECTION METHODS FOR EMERALD ASH BORER IN CANADA AND ONGOING RESEARCH ON ITS PHEROMONE CHEMICAL ECOLOGY

Krista Ryall[1], Peter J. Silk[1], Taylor Scarr[2], Loretta Shields[3], and Erin Bullas-Appleton[4]

[1]Canadian Forest Service, Great Lakes Forestry Centre, Sault Ste. Marie, ON, P6A 5E3
[2]Ontario Ministry of Natural Resources, Forests Branch, Sault Ste. Marie, ON, P6A 6V5
[3]Canadian Food Inspection Agency, Plant Health and Biosecurity Programs, St Catharines, ON L2R 5L8
[4]Canadian Food Inspection Agency, Plant Health Science Services Division,
Guelph, ON, N1G 4S9

ABSTRACT

The cryptic feeding of emerald ash borer (EAB), *Agrilus planipennis* Fairmaire (Coleoptera: Buprestidae), larvae under the bark of ash trees makes it difficult to survey and monitor for this insect. Visual surveys for signs and symptoms of EAB have been used in Canada for detection surveys since the insect was first found in Ontario in 2002 (de Groot et al. 2007, Lyons et al. 2007). Since 2010, the sensitivity of operational surveys has been improved by using branch sampling and green prism traps to detect EAB. The Canadian Food Inspection Agency (CFIA) now deploys traps (one per site) baited with (3Z)-hexenol green leaf volatile lures (de Groot et al. 2008) as part of its national survey. The traps were placed within ash tree crowns at 513 sites in 2010 and 1089 sites in 2011. The Ontario Ministry of Natural Resources (OMNR) similarly deployed an additional 30 prism traps in 2011. The traps found EAB at five new sites in 2010 (four in Ontario, one in Quebec) and three sites in 2011 (two in Ontario, one in Quebec). Operational surveys by OMNR and municipalities also use branch sampling (Ryall et al. 2011) to detect EAB. Two 5-8 cm diameter branches at the base are cut from open-grown trees. The bark and outer wood layers are whittled or stripped from the basal 50 cm of the branch to reveal EAB larval tunnels.

In 2010, branch sampling found two new infestations of EAB in Ontario (Wellington and Brant counties). Branch sampling is also used along with visual inspections to confirm an established infestation at sites where EAB has been caught in a prism trap. At two of the sites where EAB was found in Ontario in 2011 (County of Prescott and Russell and on Manitoulin Island), only a single beetle was caught in a trap. Follow-up branch sampling and visual inspections found no signs or symptoms of EAB. This presents a policy challenge as to whether a positive trap capture is sufficient evidence of an EAB infestation to justify regulatory controls.

In addition to detection surveys, branch sampling is being used by several municipalities to delimit the extent of known infestations. The manager can thus plan tree removal and injection programs by knowing which specific trees are infested. Both branch sampling and prism traps now make it more likely to find infestations within 1-2 years of EAB establishment. They can also find EAB before the trees show any symptoms of infestation. However, refinement of these techniques can increase their efficacy even further.

Silk et al. (2011) showed that the (3Z)-lactone pheromone of EAB together with (3Z)-hexenol green leaf volatiles (GLV) may increase the efficacy of prism traps. This interaction was examined in field experiments in 2011 in Ontario. The first experiment looked at whether placing green prism traps in the canopy increased efficacy. When prism traps were hung below the canopy, there was a modest increase in male EAB capture when either the GLV lure or pheromone were added, compared to blank traps. Combining the GLV lure and the pheromone in the same trap also showed only a modest increase in trap capture, with no synergism compared to either compound alone. EAB females showed consistently low trap capture and were uninfluenced by the presence of the GLV lure or the pheromone. By contrast, when the traps were placed in the tree crown, adding the GLV lure significantly increased trap capture of EAB males (doubling from a mean of ≈45 males/ blank trap to almost 100 males/ trap). Adding just the pheromone gave a modest increase in trap capture to a mean of ≈50 males/trap. Adding both the GLV lure and the pheromone to traps in the crown showed an obvious additive effect, with a mean of ≈160 males/trap. Female EAB capture rates in the canopy were slightly higher than in traps below the canopy, but again were not affected by adding or combining the GLV lure or the pheromone.

In a second field experiment, different doses of the pheromone (i.e., 0, 0.1, 1, 10, and 50 mg) were used in combination with the commercially produced GLV lure. The lowest pheromone dose of 0.1 mg was significantly most effective, catching a mean of ≈80 males/trap in the canopy. The second lowest dose (1 mg) of pheromone gave the next highest mean capture rate of ≈60 males per trap. By contrast, traps baited with just the GLV lure had a mean of about 33 males/trap. Higher pheromone doses of 10 and 50 mg had mean capture rates of approximately 45 and 43 males/trap, which were not significantly different from traps with the GLV alone. Again, female trap capture was low and unaffected by pheromone dose. The lower doses of the pheromone in the 0.1 mg range up to 1.0 mg should be explored to determine the optimum dose for capturing male EAB.

A third experiment in 2011 was done at very low EAB populations (i.e., < 2 larval galleries/m² of branch surface area). Combining the pheromone with the GLV lure almost quadrupled trap capture. Mean number of males/trap for the combination was almost 8 males/trap, compared to less than 2 males/trap for the GLV lure alone. Likewise, the number of traps that caught EAB at these very low populations was almost 90 percent when the GLV lure was combined with the pheromone. When using the GLV alone, just over 60 percent of the traps caught EAB.

These results indicate the GLV lure and pheromone work additively to increase capture of male EAB. Survey sensitivity can be enhanced even further by combining these as attractants in green prism traps hung in ash tree crowns. This tactic can also be effective at very low EAB populations. The CFIA and OMNR have incorporated this methodology as part of their detection survey plans for EAB for 2012. Future work should further refine the pheromone dose and release rate, develop a lower cost route for producing the pheromone, develop a commercial release device, and examine the interaction between female maturity, the (3Z)-lactone pheromone release, and the EAB contact pheromone.

Acknowledgments

The EAB chemical ecology work is complementary to several related projects. The contributions of Damon Crook, Ashot Krimian, and Allard Cross (USDA) are gratefully acknowledged. Jon Sweeney, Matt Lemay, Junping Wu, Peter Mayo, Hugh Evans, Jeff Fidgen, Isabelle Ochoa, and many others at the Canadian Forest Service have contributed to this work. Funding was provided by the Canadian Forest Service and through SERG-International (OMNR, Forest Protection Ltd., Manitoba, Saskatchewan, and the USFS). Troy Kimoto, CFIA survey staff, and OMNR forest health monitoring staff contributed to the surveys reported herein.

Literature Cited

de Groot, P.; Biggs, W.D.; Lyons, D.B.; Scarr, T.; Czerwinski, E.; Evans, H.J.; Ingram, W.; Marchant, K. 2007. **A visual guide for the detection of emerald ash borer.** Natural Resources Canada. 16 p.

de Groot, P.; Grant, G.G.; Poland, T.M.; Scharbach, R.; Buchan, L.; Nott, R.W.; Macdonald, L.; Pitt, D. 2008. **Electrophysiological response and attraction of emerald ash borer to green leaf volatiles (GLVs) emitted by host foliage.** Journal of Chemical Ecology. 34: 1170–1179.

Lyons, D.B.; Caister, C.; de Groot, P.; Hamilton, B.; Marchant, K.; Scarr, T.; Turgeon J. 2007. **Survey guide for detection of emerald ash borer.** Natural Resources Canada, Canadian Food Inspection Agency. 52 p.

Ryall, K.L.; Fidgen, J.G.; Turgeon, J.J. 2011. **Detectability of the emerald ash borer (Coleoptera: Buprestidae) in asymptomatic urban trees by using branch samples.** Environmental Entomology. 40: 679-688.

Silk, P.J.; Ryall, K.; Mayo, P.; Lemay, M.A.; Grant, G.; Crook, D.; Cosse, A.A.; Fraser, I.; Sweeney, J.D.; Lyons, D.B.; Pitt, D.; Scarr, T.; Magee, D. 2011. **Evidence for a volatile sex pheromone in *Agrilus planipennis* Fairmaire (Coleoptera: Buprestidae) that synergizes attraction to a host foliar volatile.** Environmental Entomology. 13: 904-916.

TREE OF HEAVEN BIOCONTROL USING INSECTS AND PATHOGENS

Amy L. Snyder[1], Matthew T. Kasson[3], Scott M. Salom[1], Donald D. Davis[3], Loke T. Kok[1], and G.J. Griffin[2]

[1]Virginia Tech, Department of Entomology, VA 24061
[2]Virginia Tech, Department of Plant Pathology, Physiology and Weed Science, Blacksburg, VA 24061
[3]The Pennsylvania State University, Department of Plant Pathology, University Park, PA 16802

ABSTRACT

Ailanthus altissima (Mill.) Swingle (Sapindales: Simaroubaceae), commonly known as tree of heaven, is an invasive tree species that has spread through much of the United States. Because of the lack of conventional control methods, biological control is being investigated as a potential control tactic for this species. Two potential biological control agents for *A. altissima* have been extensively studied: a vascular wilt fungus, *Verticillium nonalfalfae* Inderb. et al. (formerly *V. albo-atrum* Reinke and Berthold), and a host-specific weevil from China, *Eucryptorrhynchus brandti* Harold (Coleoptera: Curculionidae), which is currently pending quarantine release.

In 2002, *V. nonalfalfae* was observed in Pennsylvania causing significant mortality to *A. altissima*. From 2000 to 2008, nearly 8,000 *A. altissima* hosts died as a result (Schall and Davis 2009a). Inoculation studies have shown that this tree is highly susceptible to *V. nonalfalfae*, and resulted in 100 percent mortality of *A. altissima* greenhouse seedlings in 9 weeks and 100 percent mortality of *A. altissima* canopy trees in 3 months (Schall and Davis 2009a). Initial host-range susceptibility testing suggests *V. nonalfalfae* PSU 140 may be a low-risk biological control agent for *A. altissima*. However, risk assessment studies need to be expanded (Schall and Davis 2009b).

Eucryptorrhynchus brandti is a major pest of *A. altissima* in China and is thought to feed exclusively on this tree (Ge 2000). Adult *E. brandti* feed on leaves, stems, and petioles (Ding et al. 2006). Females oviposit eggs under the bark where the larvae feed, destroying cambial tissue until they become adults and emerge through small exit holes (Ding et al. 2006, Kok et al. 2008). In some areas of China, 80–100 percent of *A. altissima* were attacked by *E. brandti,* resulting in death for many of the trees (Ding et al. 2006, Ge 2000). Initial importation of *E. brandti* from China to the Virginia Tech Beneficial Insects Quarantine Laboratory in Blacksburg, VA in 2004 allowed for assessment of its potential as a biological control agent. Herrick et al. (2011) found *E. brandti* adults fed significantly more on North American *A. altissima* foliage in choice and no-choice feeding tests when compared with other test species. In adult oviposition tests, no evidence of *E. brandti* larvae was found in any other test species (Herrick et al. 2012). In addition, *E. brandti* has been successfully reared with high fitness for many generations (Herrick et al. 2011). These laboratory tests suggest *E. brandti* is highly host-specific and is a desirable candidate for *A. altissima* suppression.

Some herbivorous insects are able to carry plant pathogens and cause infection after feeding or contact with the host plant, and laboratory tests suggest *E. brandti* may have potential to act as a carrier for *V. nonalfalfae*. *Eucryptorrhynchus brandti* can carry propagules internally as feces after feeding on infected *A. altissima* foliage, externally by overwintering in infested potting-mix, and can initiate *A. altissima* seedling infection after external contact with the fungus. In addition, *E. brandti* were able to reproduce healthy generations on infected *A. altissima* billets. With the release of a possible long-range insect carrier, *V. nonalfalfae* may be able to spread to *A. altissima* stands otherwise unreachable for short-range pathogen dissemination (Snyder 2011).

Because of the previous documentation of *A. altissima* mortality by *V. nonalfalfae* in Pennsylvania, we wanted to: 1) evaluate the efficacy of *V. nonalfalfae* on *A. altissima*, and 2) conduct a windshield survey to find *V. nonalfalfae* infected *A. altissima* stands in Virginia, North Carolina, and South Carolina.

To evaluate the efficacy of *V. nonalfalfae* on *A. altissima*, as well as its potential for large-scale use including host specificity and performance under field conditions, *A. altissima* and 64 additional native and exotic plant species were stem-inoculated with isolate PSU140 in the field and/or greenhouse between 2006 and 2010. In 2006, only 20 canopy *A. altissima* were stem-inoculated with PSU140. By 63 months post-inoculation (MPI), nearly 9,000 *A. altissima* stems adjacent to the originally inoculated stems were either symptomatic, as evidenced by acute wilt and yellow vascular discoloration, or dead. In 2008, stem inoculations of 10 canopy *A. altissima* in two separate stands and 5 in one stand resulted in a 130–160 fold increase in diseased stems within these stands by 39 MPI, totaling 3,735 diseased *A. altissima*. In 2009, an additional *A. altissima* stand was targeted to serve as a demonstration plot to illustrate the potential effectiveness of PSU140. By 24 MPI, there was >40 fold increase of diseased trees, totaling 841 *A. altissima* from 20 inoculated stems. To date >13,000 *A. altissima* have become infected from 65 inoculated trees, a majority of which are now dead.

Recent investigations into the genetic structure of *A. altissima* populations across the United States revealed the species to be moderately diverse and sexually active, supporting the concept of multiple introductions and emphasizing the need to screen for intraspecific resistance within *A. altissima* populations in the United States. In the greenhouse, seedlings from 82 seed sources from 29 states were root inoculated with PSU140. Eleven seed sources showed resistance ranging from 8–38 percent of inoculated seedlings 14 weeks postinoculation. Of these seed sources exhibiting partial putative resistance, *V. nonalfalfae* was reisolated from three separate seed sources that exhibited only vascular discoloration.

Extended host range field testing of *V. nonalfalfae* targeted 56 native and nonnative forest associates of *A. altissima* common in south-central Pennsylvania. Closely related members of the Simaroubaceae and basally related families were inoculated in the greenhouse due to their limited geographic range within the southeastern United States. The following species were susceptible, based on acute wilt symptoms and vascular discoloration: amur corktree, autumn olive, black locust, corkwood, crossvine, elderberry, Japanese *angelica-tree*, Japanese maple, catalpa, Norway maple, poison-ivy, redbud, sassafras, staghorn sumac, and tree-of-paradise. However, only three of these species exhibited mortality following wilt: poison-ivy, redbud, and sumac. Furthermore, natural spread of *V. nonalfalfae* within diseased *A. altissima* stands was observed only for *A. altissima* and a previously tested species, striped maple (<4 percent). A third species, devil's walkingstick, acquired the disease through natural infections but no suitable stand could be found for artificial inoculations. Vascular discoloration following inoculation, but without wilt or mortality, was observed on >20 additional species. Although artificial inoculations provide an evaluation of potential damage to nontarget hosts, the low incidence of disease and mortality of these nontarget hosts among inoculated *A. altissima* offer support that PSU140 may be host adapted. Pending the outcome of host-range and molecular studies, *V. nonalfalfae* should be considered as a potential biocontrol for the invasive *Ailanthus altissima*.

A windshield survey was conducted from May to October 2011 to find *V. nonalfalfae* infected *A. altissima* stands in Virginia, North Carolina, and South Carolina. The survey was conducted on selected primary and secondary roads by visual observation of symptomatic stands. Selected symptoms included large areas of rapidly declining or dead *A. altissima*. When a stand met this criterion, individual trees were examined for vascular discoloration by removing the bark using a sterile pocketknife. If the exposed xylem contained brown streaks, a wedge of xylem was removed. Several trees per symptomatic stand were sampled. Samples were returned to the laboratory and plated on selective agar. Verification of *V. nonalfalfae* was confirmed morphologically (Hawksworth and Talboys 1970, Inderbitzin et al. 2011). Approximately 11,000 miles of primary and secondary roads in the three states were surveyed, with a focus in Virginia. At this time, the windshield survey is complete in Virginia, and we will focus on completion of North Carolina and South Carolina in summer 2012. There were 85 declining stands located. Seventy-three sites were found in Virginia, nine in North Carolina, and three in South Carolina. Six sites were found to be positive for *V. nonalfalfae* in Virginia. The largest site found contained approximately 1,000 dead, 2,500 symptomatic, and 4,000 healthy *A. altissima*.

Literature Cited

Ding, J.; Wu, Y.; Zheng, H.; Fu, W.; Reardon, R. ; Liu, M.. 2006. **Assessing potential biological control of the invasive plant, tree-of-heaven, *Ailanthus altissima*.** Biocontrol Science and Technology. 16: 547–566.

Ge, T. 2000. **Preliminary study on the biology of *Eucryptorrhynchus brandti*.** Forest Pests 2: 17–18.

Hawksworth, D.L.; Talboys, P.W. 1970. ***Verticillium albo-atrum*.** CMI descriptions of pathogenic fungi and bacteria. No. 255. Wallingford, UK: CABI Publishing.

Herrick, N.J.; Salom, S.M.; Kok, L.T.; McAvoy, T.J. 2011. **Life history, development, and rearing of *Eucryptorrynchus brandti* (Coleoptera: Curculionidae) in quarantine.** Annals of the Entomological Society of America. 104: 718–725.

Herrick, N.J., McAvoy, T.J.; Snyder, A.L.; Salom, S.M.; Kok. L.T. 2012. **Host-range testing of *Eucryptorrhynchus brandti* (Coleoptera: Curculionidae), a candidate for biological control of tree-of-heaven, *Ailanthus altissima*.** Environmental Entomology. 41: 118–124.

Inderbitzin, P.; Bostock, R.M.; Davis, R.M.; Usami, T.; Platt, H.W.; Subbarao, K. V. 2011. **Phylogenetics and taxonomy of the fungal vascular wilt pathogen *Vertcillium*, with the descriptions of five new species.** PLOS One. 6: e28341.

Kok, L.T.; Salom, S.M.; Yan, S.; Herrick, N.J.; McAvoy. T.J. 2008. **Quarantine evaluation of *Eucryptorrhynchus brandti* (Harold) (Coleoptera: Curculionidae), a potential biological control agent of tree of heaven, *Ailanthus altissima*, in Virginia USA**,. In Julien, M.H.; Sforza, R.; Bon, M.C.; Evans, H.C.; Hatcher, P.E.; Hinz H.L.; Rector B.G., eds. Proceedings, XII international symposium on biological control of weeds. Wallingford, UK: CAB International: 292–300.

Schall, M.J.; Davis; D.D. 2009a. ***Ailanthus altissima* wilt and mortality: etiology.** Plant Disease. 93: 747–751.

Schall, M.J.; Davis. D.D. 2009b. **Verticillium wilt of *Ailanthus altissima*: susceptibility of associated tree species.** Plant Disease. 93: 1158–1162.

Snyder, A.L. 2011. **Assessing *Eucryptorrhynchus brandti* as a potential carrier for *Verticillium albo-atrum* from infected *Ailanthus altissima*.** Blacksburg, VA: Virginia Tech. M.S. thesis.

IMPROVED LURES FOR EARLY DETECTION OF LONGHORN BEETLES: EFFECTS OF LURE COMBINATIONS, HOST VOLATILES, AND TRAP HEIGHT

Jon Sweeney[1], Peter J. Silk[1], Reggie Webster[1], Daniel R. Miller[2], Leland Humble[3], Krista Ryall[4], Jerzy M. Gutowski[5], Vasily Grebennikov[6], Qingfan Meng[7], Bruce Gill[6], Peter Mayo[1], Rob Johns[1], and Troy Kimoto[8]

[1]Natural Resources Canada, Canadian Forest Service, Fredericton, NB E3B 5P7
[2]U.S. Forest Service, Southern Research Station, Athens, GA 30602
[3]Natural Resources Canada, Canadian Forest Service, Victoria, BC V8Z 1M5
[4]Natural Resources Canada, Canadian Forest Service, Sault Ste. Marie, ON P6A 2E5
[5]European Centre for Natural Forests, Białowieża, Poland
[6]Canadian Food Inspection Agency, Ottawa, ON
[7]Beihua University, Jilin China
[8]Canadian Food Inspection Agency, Vancouver, BC

ABSTRACT

Long distance sex and aggregation pheromones have been discovered in many species of longhorn beetles in the last decade, especially in the subfamily Cerambycinae in which the pheromones are usually 6-, 8-, or 10-carbon hydroxy ketones or hexanediols. As Hanks et al. (2007) predicted, racemic blends of these compounds have attracted several different species of Cerambycinae and may, therefore, be useful lures for survey of longhorn beetles. Here we report results of field trapping experiments testing the efficacy of racemic 3-hydroxyhexan-2-one (C6-ketols), racemic 3-hydroxyoctan-2-one (C8-ketols), racemic $2S^*$, $3S^*$ hexanediol (S^*S^*C6-diol), and racemic $2S^*$, $3R^*$ hexanediol (S^*R^*C6-diol) for detection of longhorn species in a variety of forest habitats in Canada, Poland, China, and Russia. Our ultimate goal was to improve the suite of semiochemical lures used for surveillance and early detection of exotic bark- and wood boring beetles in North America. Objectives in 2010 and 2011 were to determine the effect of the following on the detection of longhorn species: 1) combining different pheromone lures on the same trap; 2) combining pheromone lures with a standard host volatile lure (ethanol) on the same trap; and 3) placing traps in the mid-high canopy vs. 1.5 m above the ground. No negative interactions were observed when the C6- and C8-ketols were combined on the same traps, but factorial experiments demonstrated that combining C6-ketols and S^*S^*-C6-diols significantly reduced catch of *Neoclytus acuminatus acuminatus*, *N. scutellaris*, and *N. mucronatus*. By itself, ethanol was significantly attractive to only six longhorn species, but its addition to traps baited with ketols/diols significantly enhanced mean catch of 14 species (e.g., *Phymatodes aeneus*, *Sarosesthes fulminans*) and reduced catch of only one species, *Phymatodes aereus*. Traps placed in the mid-upper canopy captured an average of 80 percent of species per site compared to only 52 percent of species detected in traps placed 1.5 m above the ground. Trap height significantly affected mean catch of 10 of 16 species. Mean catch was greater in high traps for 5/5 Lamiinae species and greater in low traps for 2/6 Cerambycinae and 2/5 Lepturinae. No one lure or lure combination performed the best at all sites, but the C6-ketols, either alone or combined with ethanol or the C8-ketols, showed the most promise for improving detection of longhorn species.

Literature Cited

Hanks, L.W.; Millar, J.G.; Moreira, J.A.; Barbour, J.D.; Lacey, E.S.; McElfresh, J.S.; Reuter, F.R.; Ray, A.M. 2007. **Using generic pheromone lures to expedite identification of aggregation pheromones for the Cerambycid Beetles** *Xylotrechus nauticus, Phymatodes lecontei,* **and** *Neoclytus modestus modestus.* Journal of Chemical Ecology. 33: 889-907.

A DIVERSE NATIVE INSECT COMMUNITY AND ITS INTERACTION WITH *SIREX NOCTILIO* IN A NORTH AMERICAN PINE FOREST

Brian M. Thompson and Daniel S. Gruner

University of Maryland, Department of Entomology, College Park, MD 20742

ABSTRACT

The invasive European woodwasp, *Sirex noctilio,* hereafter, referred to as *Sirex,* is relatively scarce in pine forests of its native European range and is considered a limited source of pine mortality. The diversity of predators, pathogens, parasitoids, and competitors in the native range of *Sirex* is thought to play an important role in *Sirex* population dynamics. In later introductions to the Southern Hemisphere where pines are not native and do not contain a diverse insect assemblage, *Sirex* populations were exponentially higher, and mortality of pine trees was likewise elevated (30-80 percent). A lack of natural enemies (enemy release hypothesis) is one postulate for why *Sirex* populations responded the way they did in the Southern Hemisphere, but the absence of competing species, as are found in the native range of *Sirex*, are conspicuously missing from explanations of Southern Hemisphere population dynamics. The recent introduction of *Sirex* to the diverse and coevolved insect communities of pine ecosystems of North America poses the question, will *Sirex* be relatively benign, as it is in its native range, or become the invasive pest it was in Southern Hemisphere locations?

Using a paired treatment design, we evaluated the potential level of interaction from insect competitors, predators, and parasitoids in a native red pine (*Pinus resinosa* Ait.) community in North America by emulating the natural attack of healthy pine trees by *Sirex*. Trees of each pairing were alternately attacked by live females, mechanically damaged, or left untouched and monitored over the course of 3 months for diversity and abundance of insect species visiting experimental treatments.

In this study, we found a strong response to *Sirex* attack of healthy trees by species known to be secondary colonizers of dying trees. Our multivariate analysis using canonical correspondence analysis with permutation tests identified the saprotrophic insect community as the only insect community with an overall positive attraction to *Sirex*-attacked trees (p=0.01). Saprotrophic species are those insects that are unable to kill healthy trees but readily make use of dead or dying trees. This specific and surprisingly rapid response among saprotrophic species was consistent across all 3 years of this study. In contrast, the response among natural enemy communities was weak and highly species dependent.

The strong response of saprotrophic species makes intuitive sense, since these species are unable to access new healthy trees as resources and must instead rely on searching out and colonizing often disparate and/or ephemeral dead or dying trees. With their rapid and direct response to aggressive tree attack by *Sirex,* saprotrophic species open the possibility for competitive and even predatory interactions and may play a key role in moderating the destructive potential of *Sirex* in North America. This study highlights the potential for diverse native communities to buffer species invasions through shared resource cues and precedes future studies on direct effects of competition on *Sirex* population dynamics.

CURRENT AND PROPOSED APHIS POLICY AND PROCESS FOR BIOLOGICAL CONTROL ORGANISMS

Robert H. Tichenor

USDA APHIS, PPQ, Riverdale, MD 20737

ABSTRACT

The policies and procedures for biological control organisms are based on the Animal and Plant Health Inspection Services (APHIS) regulations (7 CFR 330) and policies following the Plant Protection Act of 2000. There have not been substantive amendments to 7 CFR 330.200 since the 1970s. While the Plant Protection Act of 2000 contains specific language on biological control organisms, our current regulations do not, although weed biological control organisms have always fallen under 7 CFR 330. Following an internal review (2005) and recommendations from the Regulatory Change Working Group (2007-2010), new regulations are in progress (2009-2011).

Current policies regarding permitting and release of entomophagous biological control organisms (biological control of plant pests) can be broken down into four common types of biological control activities needing permits:

1. Importation of nonindigenous (often field collected) species parasites, predators, and weed biocontrol organisms for research always utilizes a containment facility; see http://www.aphis.usda.gov/plant_health/permits/organism/containment_facility_inspections.shtml for more information.

2. First time environmental release of biological control organism new to North America.

3. Interstate movement and release of weed biological control organisms, and entomophagous biocontrol organisms where not yet fully established in the United States.

4. Importation and/or interstate movement of "old"/established and "commercial" biological control organisms.

The first time environmental release of a biological control organism new to North America (#2 above) requires the following processes and documents by APHIS:

- The Petition to TAG (for Weeds) or to North American Plant Protection Organization (NAPPO) for entomophagous species

- Review of the Petition

- Recommendation to APHIS

- APHIS evaluation

- The NEPA (National Environmental Policy Act) process

- FONSI (finding of no significant impact) and release permit

The petition for entomophagous organisms must be in the form described in the regional standards for phytosanitary measures (NAPPO RSPM 12) at http://www.nappo.org/en/data/files/download/PDF/RSPM12-Rev20-10-08-e.pdf

This petition is reviewed by the Canadian Biological Control Review Committee which coordinates these reviews for the NAPPO countries using the RSPM 12 format. A recommendation from the Review Committee is sent to APHIS.

It is important to address all sections from RSPM 12, but those that should be emphasized for a successful petition are:

- 3.1 and 3.2 Taxonomy

- 3.4 Natural and expected (U.S.) geographic range

- 3.8 Known host range from literature, records, or other documentation

- 4.3 Direct impact of the biological control agent on target pest and nontarget species.

- 4.5 Indirect effects (e.g., potential impacts on organisms that depend on the target pest and nontarget species, including potential competition with resident biological control agents).

- 5 Post-release monitoring

The NEPA Process is an environmental analysis process that is conducted for organisms new to North America before they can be released into the environment. The steps in this process are:

- Review petition and forward to NAPPO Biological Control Review Committee

- Receipt and review of recommendation and comments from the NAPPO Biological Control Review Committee

- Preparation of biological assessment for Section 7 consultation with U.S. Fish and Wildlife Service

- Preparation of environmental assessment

- Tribal review evaluate and respond to public comments

- Preparation of final environmental assessment

- Reach a "Finding of no significant impact?"

- Preparation and signing of FONSI

- Continue processing of permit

It is emphasized that this set of processes from 1- 10 typically take a year or more from submission of the petition to issuance of the permit. Additional information that may be needed after review by the Biological Control Review Committee or after comments during the tribal or public reviews of the environmental assessment obviously could lengthen that time frame.

Details and advice about the information needed for submission of these forms and assistance with the permitting processes can be obtained by calling 301-524-5421 or on line at http://www.aphis.usda.gov/permits/ppq_epermits.shtml, or contacting me directly.

These future regulations require the promulgation of the above policies and implementation of the authorities regarding containment of regulated organisms. APHIS is contemplating the proposal of regulations based on organism risk. As such biological control organisms would be divided up into three administrative categories with the lowest risk category being those that are fully established in the environment and have not been known to cause adverse nontarget or environmental effects. A second category would be for those that have gone through the full environmental review process described above, but for which establishment and nontarget monitoring and documentation is still ongoing. The third category would be all other biological control organisms, including those still requiring containment.

BIOLOGICAL CONTROL FOR THE PROTECTION OF BIODIVERSITY IN NATURAL SYSTEMS

Roy Van Driesche

University of Massachusetts, Department of Plant, Soil &
Insect Sciences/Entomology, Amherst, MA, 01003

ABSTRACT

Biological control of weeds and pest insects that invade natural areas have contributed to the protection of the biodiversity of many native ecosystems. Additional benefits of such biological control efforts in natural areas include the preservation of wildlands as sources of timber or other renewable resources, maintenance of these ecosystems as recreational areas, and protection of some ecosystem services such as flood control, fire regulation, and maintenance of healthy soils.

Many examples exist of invasive plants whose impacts in natural areas (forests, grasslands, wetlands, bodies of water) have been reduced by the importation of natural enemies of the plants. Wetland communities, which have in many cases been dramatically modified by invasions of exotic plants, are a case in point. One such example is the protection of a range of habitats in southern Florida, including plant communities in the Everglades (a World Heritage site) and adjacent cypress forests that were threatened with fundamental physical alteration and biological impoverishment by the invasive tree *Melaleuca quinquenervia* (Cav.) Blake. Several introduced insects, especially the melaleuca weevil (*Oxyops vitiosa* Pascoe) and the meleuca psyllid (*Boreioglycaspis melaleucae* [Moore]), have successfully "neutered" the tree, denying it the ability to spread into new areas by destroying seed protection and lowering survival of seedlings and stump sprouts. This now allows physical removal of large stems without rapid recolonization from seed banks or recovery through stump sprouting. Since 1993, the area in southern Florida infested with this tree has been reduced in half. Habitats where melaleuca density has declined have been recolonized by a mix of largely native plants, representing substantial ecosystem recovery. Also, in the absence of melaleuca, soil accretion is reduced, and fire intensity in habitats is lowered. More broadly, around the world in the twentieth century, 40 species of invasive plants have been suppressed in this manner, many of which likely have contributed to the restoration of the biodiversity of the systems these plants invaded.

Biological control of invasive insects that affect forest trees or other plants in parks, forest reserves, or the general landscape also has contributed to the protection of plant biodiversity, as well as the biodiversity of the arthropods that are specialized feeders on the affected plants. One such example of the protection afforded to native plants from insect biological control is the suppression of the cottony cushion scale (*Icerya purchasi* Maskell) in the Galápagos National Park of Ecuador. This polyphagous scale feeds on and damages over 60 species of native Galápagan plants, about half of which are local endemics. Many of these latter are rare and endangered species with small distributions and are quite valuable for their contribution to world plant biodiversity, as well as their role in the local maintenance of Galápagos ecosystems. Not only are these rare plants of interest in their own right, but many are also the required hosts for rare insects or snails that depend on these plants for survival. Release of the coccinellid *Rodolia cardinalis* (Mulsant) on these islands in 2002 suppressed this scale on most plants and concretely benefitted 16 threatened plant species, as well as many other native plants that were being damaged by this scale. One such rare plant was *Darwiniothamnus tenuifolius* (Hook. F.) Harling whose reduction in some locations is believed to have caused local population extirpations of three rare moths. Ecological benefits from this biological control project also included protection of some species of mangroves. For example, white mangrove (*Laguncularia racemosa* L.) on Santa Cruz Island was heavily damaged by cottony cushion scale before 2002 but is now virtually scale free and in good health. Recovered mangrove stands are now again able to provide essential habitat for marine species and nesting habitat for the critically endangered mangrove finch, *Camarhynchus heliobates* Snodgrass & Heller, on the island of Isabela.

The role of classical biological control in protecting biodiversity of native ecosystems and the stability of natural habitats is an emerging focus. Increased cooperation between biological control scientists and conservation biologists is needed to better integrate such efforts into the framework of conservation biology.

PREDATION STUDIES OF *LARICOBIUS OSAKENSIS* MONTGOMERY AND SHIYAKE (COLEOPTERA: DERODONTIDAE), A PREDATOR OF HEMLOCK WOOLLY ADELGID, *ADELGES TSUGAE* ANNAND (HEMIPTERA: ADELGIDAE)

Ligia C. Vieira, Scott M. Salom, and Loke T. Kok

Virginia Tech, Department of Entomology, Blacksburg, VA 24061

ABSTRACT

Hemlock woolly adelgid, *Adelges tsugae* Annand (Hemiptera: Adelgidae), an introduced pest from Japan, is threatening eastern (*Tsuga canadensis* (L.) Carrière) and Carolina (*T. caroliniana* Engelmann) hemlock forests in the eastern United States. This pest can colonize all hemlock species and is relatively innocuous for Asian and western U.S. hemlock species but can be fatal to eastern and Carolina hemlocks.

Considering the wide geographic distribution of *A. tsugae* and its high fecundity, the biological control strategy for this pest has focused on establishing a natural enemy complex that can impact *A. tsugae* populations for each stage of development and also be adapted to the various environmental conditions where the pest is present. So far, three species of predators have been released for the control of *A. tsugae*: *Sasajiscymnus tsugae* Sasaji and McClure (Coleoptera: Coccinellidae), *Laricobius nigrinus* Fender (Coleoptera: Derodontidae), and *Scymnus sinuanodulus* Yu and Yao (Coleoptera: Coccinellidae). Encouraging results from releases of *L. nigrinus*, a specialized predator of *A. tsugae* from western North America, has created considerable interest in *L. osakensis* Montgomery & Shiyake, a congeneric predator first found in association with *A. tsugae* in Japan in 2005. *L. osakensis* was found to be a key predator of *A. tsugae* in its native range, and like *L. nigrinus*, was also found to be a highly specialized predator. In June 2010, this predator received a finding of no significant impact from the U.S. Department of Agriculture Animal and Plant Health Inspection Service (USDA APHIS), allowing this species to be removed from quarantine and more fully evaluated as a potential biological control agent.

The success of a biological control program is usually evaluated by the impact an introduced natural enemy has in keeping the pest population at a low, less-damaging level. Laboratory studies and cage field studies on feeding and reproduction can provide insight on the potential of a given predator to impact the pest population. These studies were carried out to evaluate the potential of *L. osakensis* to suppress *A. tsugae* populations. Functional and numerical responses of *L. osakensis* and *L. nigrinus* to *A. tsugae* were assessed in the laboratory. Additionally, the survivorship, feeding, and reproduction of *L. osakensis* were also evaluated in the field.

Functional response is the change in feeding rate, and numerical response is the change in the predator population (reproduction and migration) in response to changes in prey density. The assay for predator adults (males and females) or larvae consisted of containers with predetermined densities (3, 6, 12, 24, and 48) of *A. tsugae* ovisacs that were exposed to one individual predator for 3 or 7 days, respectively. The number of ovisacs consumed and eggs laid were recorded at the end of this period. The functional response of adults (males and females) and larvae of both species followed a Type II response. The overall attack rates and handling times for *L. osakensis* males and females were similar. Attack rates for *L. nigrinus* males and females were similar, but handling times differed significantly. Attack rates and handling times for females of both species were similar, but *L. nigrinus* males had both a greater attack rate and handling time than *L. osakensis*. When only considering *A. tsugae* adults killed, males of both species killed significantly more prey adults than females. Numerical response was measured as the number of eggs laid by the females. *L. osakensis* females showed a greater numerical response than *L. nigrinus*. Females laid eggs in several locations, with *L. osakensis* preferring to lay the eggs under the adelgid while *L. nigrinus* preferred to lay the eggs in the wool. For the larvae, *L. osakensis* handling time was significantly less than *L. nigrinus*, while the attack rate was similar. The greater numerical response of *L. osakensis* combined with the greater functional response of *L. osakensis* larvae indicates this predator can be potentially more effective in the control of *A. tsugae* populations.

Long-term (2 months) and short-term (15 days) cage studies were conducted to evaluate survival, reproduction, and impact of this predator in Saltville, VA. For each sampling period, four branches from each of five trees received one of two treatments: caged hemlock branches with predators, or caged hemlock branches without predators. *L. osakensis* adults survived from December to April. Survivorship was affected by the climatic conditions, degree of disturbance during the

trial, and prey availability. Females laid eggs during the entire sampling period, with the highest numbers being laid during March and April. Females produced up to a maximum of 34 eggs during a 15-day period. Adelgid densities on branches with predators were significantly lower than branches without predators in all sampling periods. The difference was especially significant in the long-term cages where the impact of both adults and larvae was observed. In all long-term branches with predators, no hemlock woolly adelgid adult survived, and only a maximum of 2 ovisacs (all eggs) were not completely consumed. All long-term branches without predators had some percentage of *A. tsugae* adults alive, and all ovisacs were undisturbed. In the long-term cages with predators where enough prey was available, larvae were able to complete development. *L. osakensis* can survive, feed, and reproduce in Saltville, VA.

Laboratory and field studies indicate *L. osakensis* can be a promising addition to the natural enemy complex, potentially exerting a greater impact in hemlock woolly adelgid populations than *L. nigrinus*.

EVALUATION OF INSECTICIDE EFFICACY IN ASIAN LONGHORNED BEETLE ERADICATION PROGRAMS

Baode Wang and Victor C. Mastro

USDA APHIS, PPQ, CPHST, Buzzards Bay, MA, 02542

ABSTRACT

We briefly reviewed the development of using insecticides for the prophylactic treatment of host trees and the effectiveness of the treatments in the eradication programs for the Asian longhorned beetle (ALB), *Anoplophora glabripennis*, in the United States.

Most of the field efficacy evaluations were conducted in several locations in China with cooperators from the Chinese Academy of Forestry, Beijing Forestry University, and the University of Science and Technology of China, as well as with participants from a number of local institutions.

Animal and Plant Health Inspection Service (APHIS) started evaluation of insecticides for ALB control and as prophylactic treatments in 1997. Field efficacy tests were conducted in subsequent years. Insecticides used as cover sprays, including pyrethroids, acephate, chlorpyrifos, lindane, bendiocarb, carbaryal, and fipronil, were tested for efficacy against adult beetles feeding on twigs of treated plants. Generally, most of the above listed insecticides had a very good short term efficacy. However, their efficacies were greatly reduced after 2 weeks, especially for the pyrethroid insecticides that were not encapsulated.

Various systemic insecticides in the classes of organochlorine, organophosphorus, carbamate, macrocyclic lactone, neonicotinyl, and botanical were tested through tree trunk injection, soil injection, or trunk implanting. The insecticide treatments were applied at different times of the year, and some selected insecticides were applied at different doses and with different trunk or soil delivery methods. The efficacies of these insecticide treatments were evaluated based on the mortality of caged and wild adult beetles feeding on treated trees, the number of new exit holes, and their behaviors on treated trees. Mortalities of immature stages of the beetles were compared for different treatments based on the mortality data collected from dissecting treated trees either in late October, early November, or late spring.

Although the efficacy for the same active ingredient varied because of the application timing, formulations, and delivery methods as well as other factors, the following conclusions can still be generalized:

- Systemic organophosphorus and carbamate insecticides that we tested were generally less effective than imidacloprid through either tree trunk injection, or soil injection.

- When considering both current year and residual efficacy, imidacloprid (through tree trunk and soil injection) generally is the best choice for controlling ALB.

- Efficacy of acetamiprid (though soil and trunk injection), thiacloprid (through trunk injection), and clothiandin (through trunk injection) may be comparable to imidacloprid treatment.

- Although dinotefuran was in some cases less efficacious than imidacloprid and acetamiprid for ALB adults, the insecticide is more water soluble and can be used to inject into tree trunks for quick kill of ALB adults when necessary.

The LC_{50} and LC_{90} values for imidacloprid, dinotefuran, clothianidin, and thiamethoxam were determined for ALB. We also conducted a field study to determine whether ALB adults can detect sublethal amounts of imidacloprid and, therefore, avoid feeding on and move away from treated trees. The results showed that beetles placed on imidacloprid treated trees moved much less frequently to another tree than the beetles placed on untreated trees did. Most of adults remained on the treated trees until they were dead.

We planted uninfested willow trees amongst heavily infested willow trees in the spring of 2008 to assess the efficacy of imidacloprid treatment for protecting trees from infestation in an area with high ALB population, similar to the core ALB infestation areas in the United States. Two thirds of these newly planted trees were treated with imidacloprid through tree trunk injection 2 weeks before the estimated adult emergence. Half of the imidacloprid treated trees were treated again in 2009. Although a few feeding sites were found, there were very few egg pits, and subsequent inspections have not found any ALB exit holes on any of the willow trees treated for 2 years The results of this study demonstrated that imidacloprid treatment can protected trees even in high ALB density areas.

In the United States, the ALB program reported that of the nearly 250,000 exposed trees treated in NY, IL, and NJ, there was firm evidence in only six cases of oviposition in the year of treatment and successful emergence the following year. In all cases, it occurred after a single treatment. ALB program-wide, only 0.004 percent of imidacloprid treated trees were found to have either live larvae or adult emergences.

SWALLOW-WORTS (*VINCETOXICUM*): FIRST PETITION FOR BIOCONTROL RELEASE

Aaron Weed, Richard Casagrande, Alex Hazlehurst, and Lisa Tewksbury

University of Rhode Island, Department of Plant Sciences and Entomology, Kingston, RI 02881

ABSTRACT

A classical biological control program has been initiated against the invasive European swallow-worts *Vincetoxicum nigrum* and *V. rossicum* in North America since 2001. Of the five biological control agents that have been under evaluation since 2006, the leaf-feeding moth *Hypena opulenta* is the most promising. *Hypena opulenta* is multivoltine and should produce at least two generations per year in North America. Larvae feed primarily on newly developing foliage, and damage by two larvae per plant can reduce *Vincetoxicum* growth and reproduction. We evaluated the host range of *H. opulenta* on 79 plant species within 10 families. The majority of plant species were North American, but many nonnative species of economic importance were also screened. In these tests, larvae of *H. opulenta* only completed development on *Vincetoxicum,* averaging over 75 percent survival on both target weeds. Some feeding and partial development occurred on two plants in the Urticaceae, but larvae never completed development to pupation on these species. Our studies conclude that *H. opulenta* poses little risk to North American plants and is a promising biological control agent of *Vincetoxicum*. We have petitioned for the release of *H. opulenta* for the upcoming field season in 2012.

In preparation for field releases of *H. opulenta*, populations of *V. nigrum* and *V. rossicum* have been monitored since 2008 on Naushon Island, Massachusetts. Monitoring plots were established in patches of both species and within open and forested patches of *V. rossicum*. Our monitoring plots will allow us to evaluate how multiple factors (plant species and sun exposure) affect the establishment and impact of *H. opulenta* when we are granted the permission to release.

We have also demonstrated in other studies that the host range of another leaf-feeding moth, *Abrostola asclepiadis*, is also restricted to *Vincetoxicum*. We will delay petitioning for the release of *A. asclepiadis* until evaluation of *H. opulenta* releases are completed.

THE EFFECT OF BARK THICKNESS ON PARASITISM OF TWO EMERALD ASH BORER PARASITOIDS: *TETRASTICHUS PLANIPENNISI* AND *ATANYCOLUS* SPP.

Kristopher J. Abell[1,2], Leah S. Bauer[2,3], Jian J. Duan[4], Jonathan P. Lelito[5], and Roy Van Driesche[1]

[1]University of Massachusetts, Department of Plant, Soil & Insect Sciences, Amherst, MA 01003
[2]Michigan State University, Department of Entomology, East Lansing, MI 48824
[3]U.S. Forest Service, Northern Research Station, East Lansing, MI 48823
[4]USDA ARS, Beneficial Insects Introduction Research Unit, Newark DE 45433
[5]USDA APHIS PPQ, EAB Biological Control Facility, Brighton, MI 48116

ABSTRACT

The emerald ash borer (EAB), *Agrilus planipennis* Fairmaire (Coleoptera: Buprestidae), is an invasive wood-boring beetle from Asia that is killing ash trees (*Fraxinus* spp.) in North America. The larval parasitoid *Tetrastichus planipennisi* Yang (Hymenoptera: Eulophidae) is one of three EAB parasitoid species from China being released for biological control of EAB in the United States. Recent studies in Michigan show increasing parasitism of EAB larvae by species of *Atanycolus* (Hymenoptera: Braconidae), which are native ectoparasitoids of *Agrilus* larvae.

At EAB biocontrol study sites in central Michigan, EAB larval parasitism by *T. planipennisi* is more common in smaller than in larger diameter ash trees, whereas *Atanycolus* is unaffected by tree diameter. Since parasitoids of wood-boring insects must drill into tree trunks, ovipositor length, bark thickness, and host depth affect their ability to reach and successfully parasitize hosts. We evaluated the effect of bark thickness on EAB larval parasitism by *T. planipennisi* (ovipositor length range = 2.0 to 2.5 mm) and *Atanycolus* (ovipositor length range = 4 to 6 mm).

In spring 2011, we grafted EAB eggs onto trunks of small and large green ash trees (*F. pennsylvanica*). Later in the summer, we caged either *T. planipennisi* or *Atanycolus* adults on tree trunks where the EAB larvae were feeding. When the larvae were mature in the fall, we debarked the lower tree trunks, measured the thickness of the outer bark, and collected the larvae to determine parasitism. We found *T. planipennisi* parasitized EAB larvae in green ash trees up to 11.2 cm in diameter at breast height (d.b.h.), which correlates to outer bark thicknesses up to 3.2 mm. *Atanycolus* parasitized EAB larvae in ash trees up to 57.4 cm d.b.h., which correlates to outer bark thicknesses up to 8.8 mm. These results indicate that establishment and spread of *T. planipennisi* is more likely at release sites dominated by small, early successional or regenerating ash trees than at sites with only large, mature ash trees. Moreover, this study demonstrates that sustainable term management of EAB in North America will require a diverse natural enemy complex including native parasitoids, which may become important allies in controlling EAB.

DEVELOPMENT OF EMERALD ASH BORER (*AGRILUS PLANIPENNIS*) IN NOVEL ASH (*FRAXINUS* SPP.) HOSTS

Andrea C. Anulewicz[1] and Deborah G. McCullough[1,2]

[1]Michigan State University, Department of Entomology, East Lansing, MI 48824
[2]Michigan State University, Department of Forestry, East Lansing, MI 48824

ABSTRACT

Emerald ash borer (EAB), *Agrilus planipennis* Fairmaire, has successfully colonized every ash species (*Fraxinus* spp.) it has encountered in eastern forests and urban areas, including green ash (*F. pennsylvanica* Marsh.), white ash (*F. Americana* L.), black ash (*F. nigra* Marsh.), blue ash (*F. quadrangulata* Michx.), pumpkin ash (*F. profunda* [Bush] Bush), and a number of commercially available hybrids. The range of ash spans the continent of North America, and widespread devastation by the emerald ash borer, similar to that in southern Michigan and northern Ohio, could potentially occur. In addition to several nonnative species used in landscapes, there are at least 11 other ash species native to North America. Susceptibility of these species to EAB is unknown. If one or more of these species proves to be resistant, then we may be able to identify and enhance resistance mechanisms. Furthermore, information about the relative susceptibility of ash species to EAB could help municipal foresters, natural resource managers, and regulatory officials plan for the arrival of EAB in their region.

In spring 2008 and 2009, we established a plantation with three European ash species, including European ash (*F. excelsior* L.), flowering ash (*F. ornus* L.), and Raywood ash (*F. oxycarpa* 'Raywood'), the Asian species Manchurian ash (*F. mandshurica* Rupr.), the tropical species *F. uhdei* (Wenzig) Lingelsh., and four North American ash species, including green ash, blue ash, Oregon ash (*F. latifolia* Benth.), and velvet ash (*F. velutina* Torr.), along with privet (*Ligustrum vulgare* L.), a close relative of ash. Two of the North American species are native to western states, and EAB populations have not yet encountered these species. In addition to the plantation, in spring 2010, we acquired five species of Asian ash seedlings propagated from seed harvested in China and Japan (*F. insularis* Hemsl., *F. lanuginose* Koidz., *F. mandshurica*, *F. paxiana* Lingelsh., and *F. stylosa* Lingelsh.) by colleagues at the Morton Arboretum. These seedlings were maintained in pots in a lath house. Our objectives were to determine: (1) if adult EAB will feed on foliage of novel ash species and, if so, evaluate their longevity; and (2) whether female EAB will oviposit on novel ash species and, if so, evaluate larval survival and development.

To assess adult leaf feeding, we constructed cages that enabled EAB adults to feed on intact ash leaves. Two male and two female EAB were placed into each cage and allowed to feed for 4 days. Each leaf was removed and scanned to determine the area consumed by beetles. To assess adult mortality, beetles used in the intact leaf-feeding bioassays were moved to new leaves on the same tree and allowed to feed for an additional 10 days (14 days total). Cages and beetles were moved to new leaves twice per week, and beetle mortality was recorded each time.

Trees in the plantation were left undisturbed and exposed to wild EAB populations. In summer 2011, we carefully inspected each tree in the plantation to assess EAB infestation rates prior to 2011. We surveyed the entire tree for EAB emergence holes and woodpecker attacks on late instar larvae. Additional plant health parameters were also measured, but are not presented here. Adult EAB emergence holes and woodpecker attacks were stapled, enabling us to track EAB infestation rates from year to year.

Adult EAB fed to some degree on foliage from all species tested. Beetles consumed twice as much leaf area on velvet ash and four of the Asian ash species as they did on the other ash species, but few beetles survived for 14 days on velvet ash and Asian ashes. Larval EAB developed successfully on all species tested, except privet. We recorded EAB emergence holes on five previously undocumented host species, including Oregon ash and velvet ash, native to the west coast and southwestern United States, respectively, flowering ash and Raywood ash, both native to Europe, and tropical ash, native to Mexico.

EFFICACY OF TWO TRAPPING TECHNIQUES FOR LARGE WOODBORING BEETLES IN SOUTHERN PINE STANDS

Brittany F. Barnes[1], Daniel R. Miller[2], Christopher M. Crowe[2], and Kamal J.K Gandhi[1]

[1]The University of Georgia, Daniel B. Warnell School of Forestry and Natural Resources, Athens, GA 30602
[2]U.S Forest Service, Southern Research Station, Athens GA 30602

ABSTRACT

In the United States, surveys on woodboring beetles (Coleoptera: Cerambycidae and Buprestidae) are conducted annually to detect new exotic species. Typically, Lindgren funnel traps and intercept panel traps baited with various lures are used in these surveys to catch bark and woodboring beetles. Trapping efficiency of these two trap types have been studied, but little is known about how they could be modified in terms of lure placement to increase the number and diversity of woodboring beetles in traps.

During June-August 2010, we established 10 replicates of three traps per block in a mature loblolly pine (*Pinus taeda* L.) stand in the Oconee National Forest, Georgia. Traps were baited with a combination of ethanol, α-pinene, and racemic ipsenol and ipsdienol. Three trap types were used as follows: 1) intercept panel trap; 2) modified funnel trap with lures placed on the inside of trap; and 3) modified funnel trap with lures placed on the outside of trap. Funnel traps were modified by increasing the diameter of the center from 5.5 to 12 cm, so that the lures could fit in the trap.

A total of 2,145 beetles in three different woodboring beetle families (Cerambycidae, Buprestidae, and Elateridae) and 24 different species were captured. Twice as many beetles were caught in the funnel traps with the lures placed on the inside when compared to the other two trap types. None of the beetle species preferred the lures placed on the outside of the funnel traps, and only one elaterid beetle species (*Alaus myops* F.) preferred the panel trap over the funnel traps. Species richness was higher in funnel traps with lures placed on the inside. Species composition differed among the three trap types such that funnel traps with the lure placed on the inside and panel traps were on opposite ends of the hypothetical gradient. We concluded that funnel traps with the lures placed on the inside will likely maximize the catches and diversity of woodboring beetles however; different species may be caught in these three trap types.

DETERMINING ESTABLISHMENT AND PREVALENCE OF PARASITOIDS RELEASED FOR BIOLOGICAL CONTROL OF THE EMERALD ASH BORER

Leah S. Bauer[1,2], Jian J. Duan[3], Juli Gould[4], Kristopher J. Abell[2,6], Jason Hansen[4], Jonathan P. Lelito[5], and Roy Van Driesche[6]

[1]U.S. Forest Service, Northern Research Station, East Lansing, MI 48823
[2]Michigan State University, Department of Entomology, East Lansing, MI 48824
[3]USDA ARS, Beneficial Insects Introduction Research Unit, Newark, DE 45433
[4]USDA APHIS, Center for Plant Health Science and Technology, Buzzards Bay, MA 02542
[5]USDA APHIS PPQ, EAB Biological Control Facility, Brighton, MI 48116
[6]University of Massachusetts, Department of Plant, Soil & Insect Sciences, Amherst, MA 01003

ABSTRACT

The emerald ash borer (EAB), (*Agrilus planipennis* Fairmaire), an invasive buprestid from Asia, is causing widespread mortality of ash trees in North America. Classical biological control of EAB in the United States started in 2007 with the release of three hymentopteran parasitoids from China: *Oobius agrili* Zhang and Huang (Encyrtidae), *Tetrastichus planipennisi* Yang (Eulophidae), and *Spathius agrili* Yang (Braconidae). Release of these species started at study sites in Michigan and has since expanded to the other EAB-infested states. Using destructive and nondestructive sampling methods, establishment of at least one of these parasitoid species is confirmed in Michigan, Ohio, Indiana, Illinois, and Maryland.

Different methods are needed for detection of egg vs. larval parasitoids. The egg parasitoid *O. agrili* can be detected in the field by 1) sampling EAB eggs from bark of EAB-infested ash trees and determining which eggs are parasitized; 2) rearing *O. agrili* from bark or log samples in the laboratory; and 3) hanging egg-sentinel logs (ESLs, small ash logs on which EAB eggs were laid) on ash trees. Using ESLs, we have tracked *O. agrili* parasitism seasonally and spatially since 2009 at higher prevalence than determined by other detection methods. The larval parasitoids *T. planipennisi* and *S. agrili* can be detected in the field by: 1) debarking infested ash trees and assessing parasitism of each larva; 2) rearing adult wasps from ash logs in the laboratory; 3) hanging larval-sentinel logs (LSLs, small ash logs in which EAB larvae were inserted) on ash trees; and 4) placing yellow pan traps (YPTs) on ash trees in late summer or fall to catch adult parasitoids, which are later identified. Tree debarking provides the most data on parasitoid species attacking EAB larvae, however, LSLs and YPTs may be useful for detecting the presence of adult larval parasitoids if ash trees are too scarce to sample.

LABORATORY BIOASSAY OF EMERALD ASH BORER ADULTS WITH A *BACILLUS THURINGIENSIS* FORMULATION SPRAYED ON ASH LEAVES

Leah S. Bauer[1,2], Deborah L. Miller[1], and Diana Londoño[2]

[1]U.S. Forest Service, Northern Research Station, East Lansing, MI 48823
[2]Michigan State University, Department of Entomology, East Lansing, MI 48824

ABSTRACT

The emerald ash borer (EAB), (*Agrilus planipennis* Fairmaire), is an invasive buprestid from Asia causing extensive mortality of ash trees (*Fraxinus* spp.) in areas of North America. For sustainable management of EAB, a classical biological control program began in Michigan in 2007 with the release of three hymenopteran parasitoids of EAB from China. Biocontrol has since expanded to other EAB-infested states. Given the high population densities of EAB and the limited resistance of North America ash species to it, more management methods are needed to assure survival and recovery of *Fraxinus* spp. To this end, we are working to develop a microbial insecticide made from the insect-pathogenic bacterium *Bacillus thuringiensis* (Bt) strain SDS-502, which is toxic to EAB adults. Due to the narrow host range of Bt, this bacterium is used worldwide to control specific insect pests in agricultural, riparian, and forested ecosystems (e.g., aerial sprays to control gypsy moth), and after decades of use, it continues to have a good safety record with respect to human health and the environment.

Previously, we reported on the toxicity and mode of action of Bt SDS-502 in EAB adults, the lack of Bt toxicity in adult hymenopteran parasitoids, and the efficacy of Bt-test formulations sprayed on ash leaves and fed to EAB adults. We now report on the mortality response of EAB adults to three concentrations of a wettable, dispersible granular (WDG) formulation of Bt SDS-502 (Bt-WDG contained 50 percent Bt-technical powder, Lot #PHY-3-11) sprayed using a rotary atomizer (Micronair ULVA+). One-mL aliquots of each Bt concentration (25, 50, 100 mg Bt-WDG /mL 10 percent sucrose solution) were pipetted into the sprayer reservoir, sprayed on greenhouse-grown ash leaves (*F. uhdei*), and fed to EAB adults. After 7 d, observed EAB mortality was 20, 43, and 50 percent at each concentration, respectively, whereas control mortality was <3 percent for the WDG-blank formulation and 10 percent sucrose. Time to death averaged 4.3 d and was similar at the three Bt-WDG concentrations. By increasing the concentration of Bt SDS-502 in the formulation and designing a formulation for aerial application, we anticipate higher levels of EAB adult mortality in the laboratory. Once this is achieved, further testing of the formulation in the field will be needed.

A NEW SYNTHESIS AND LURE FOR (+)-DISPARLURE

John H. Borden, Ervin Kovacs, and J.P. Lafontaine

Contech Enterprises Inc., Delta, BC, V4G 1E9

ABSTRACT

We have developed a proprietary new synthesis for (+)-disparlure that involves a novel method of ensuring extremely high enantiomeric purity. When analyzed by the U.S. Department of Agriculture Animal and Plant Health Inspection Service (USDA APHIS), the synthetic pheromone was determined to have 96 percent and 99.8 percent chemical and optical purity, respectively. When tested in the field by USDA APHIS, catches in traps baited with the USDA standard pheromone on dental cotton wicks fell off steeply at high doses, indicating repellence due to increasing levels of (-)-disparlure, whereas catches in traps baited with the new synthetic pheromone fell off only slightly. The new synthetic pheromone was formulated into PVC flexlures which provide easier handling than string lures. When tested in the field in Wisconsin, catches in Unitraps baited with Contech flexlures or Trécé string lures were not significantly different, and both were significantly higher than catches in traps baited with Hercon strip lures or Scentry grey rubber septa. An experiment designed to test a new plastic bag trap baited with Contech flexlures showed that it was far inferior to Unitraps baited with the same lure. In this experiment, delta traps baited with Contech flexlures caught the expected number of approximately 10 males per trap, about the same number as Safer bag traps, a retail product that proved to be poorly designed to mass trap males. Insertion of a 1 cm^2 block of Vapona into the experimental bag trap significantly improved catches, demonstrating that escapes occurred through the side entry ports. Our results indicate that we have met our two most important objectives of: 1) developing a new synthesis that produces (+)-disparlure of the highest quality, and 2) formulating the new synthetic pheromone into a lure that is competitive with the best alternative lure currently available.

LETHAL TRAP TREES: A POTENTIAL TOOL FOR MANAGING EMERALD ASH BORER

Jacob Bournay[1,2], Deborah G. McCullough[1,2], Nicholas J. Gooch[1],
Andrea C. Anulewicz[1], and Phillip A. Lewis[3]

[1]Michigan State University, Department of Entomology, East Lansing, MI 48824
[2]Michigan State University, Department of Forestry, East Lansing, MI 48824
[3]USDA APHIS, PPQ, CPHST, Buzzards Bay, MA 02542

ABSRACT

Tactics to help slow emerald ash borer (EAB), *Agrilus planipennis* Fairmaire, population growth could delay the onset and progression of ash mortality, particularly in localized outlier sites. Previous studies have shown adult EAB, including ovipositing females, are highly attracted to *Fraxinus* spp. trees that have been intentionally girdled. Girdled ash trees can be used for EAB detection and can function as population "sinks" if larvae in the tree are destroyed before they complete development. Removal or destruction of infested, girdled trees, however, can be costly and labor intensive.

The insecticide product sold as TREE-äge™ with the active ingredient emamectin benzoate (EB) provided nearly 100 percent control of EAB for 2 years in a large-scale field study. We hypothesized that injecting trees with emamectin benzoate, then girdling trees 2-3 weeks later, could effectively create lethal trap trees. Volatiles emitted by the girdled trees would presumably attract adult EAB, but the insecticide would control leaf-feeding adults, larval EAB, or both life stages.

In 2009 and again in 2010, we used a block design replicated at three sites to compare densities of EAB larvae on similarly-sized ash trees. Each block consisted of four trees that were randomly assigned to be left as untreated controls (C), girdled (G), injected with TREE-äge™ (EB), or injected and subsequently girdled (EB+G). Trees were felled and debarked in autumn of each year to quantify larval density.

Results from both 2009 and 2010 showed there were almost no live larvae in either the trees injected with TREE-äge™, even those that were girdled 3 weeks after injection (EB+G). Larval density was significantly and substantially higher on girdled trees and untreated controls than on the EB and EB+G trees in both years. In 2010, residues of emamectin benzoate averaged (± SE) 5.8 ±1.40 and 5.6 ±1.23 ppm, respectively, in leaves from EB and EB+G trees. This shows the product was effectively translocated to the canopy, despite the girdling that was applied 3 weeks after the insecticide was injected. In bioassays with adult EAB, 90-100 percent of beetles died by Day 3 when caged with leaves from the EB or EB+G trees, compared to <10 percent EAB mortality on C and G trees. Analysis of foliar residues and adult EAB bioassay data from 2011 is underway. Overall, results indicate that lethal trap trees are effective and could be useful as an option in integrated management programs to slow EAB population growth and ash mortality.

COMPARISON OF NATIVE AND EXOTIC SUBCORTICAL BEETLE COMMUNITIES AROUND WAREHOUSES AND NURSERIES IN GEORGIA

Kayla A. Brownell[1], Mark Raines[2], Terry Price[2], Chip Bates[3], and Kamal J.K. Gandhi[1]

[1]University of Georgia, Warnell School of Forestry and Natural Resources, Athens, GA 30602
[2]Georgia Forestry Commission, Waynesboro, GA 30830
[3]Georgia Forestry Commission, Athens, GA 30605

ABSTRACT

Subcortical beetles such as buprestid (Buprestidae), cerambycid (Cerambycidae), and scolytine (Curculionidae) beetles are commonly found in forest communities and assist in the breakdown of woody debris and nutrient cycling. Warehouses and nurseries may be potential introduction sites for invasive species because of buildup of introduced host material. The two objectives of this study were to assess differences between nonnative subcortical beetle communities around warehouses and nurseries and to assess the response of those communities to lures commonly used in national surveys. Beetles were trapped between April and August 2010 at seven sites in Georgia. Three survey sites were located at warehouses and four at nurseries. Beetles were trapped every 14-15 days using 12-unit Lindgren funnel traps with a wet collection cup. Each trap had one of the following, randomly selected, lure combinations: a) Ultra High Release (UHR) ethanol, b) UHR ethanol + UHR α-pinene, and c) exotic *Ips* lure. All adult beetles (4,093 in total) were identified to species-level using available literature. Only scolytine species accounted for >5 percent of the total beetle catches, and exotic scolytine species dominated the fauna at these sites. There were no significant differences in total beetle catches between sites and among lure types for the exotic beetle species. However, at species-level, although there were still no significant differences between sites and among lure types, some trends are evident. *Xylosandrus crassiusculus* (Motschulsky) was the most commonly intercepted species. Almost 15 times more *X. crassiusculus* were trapped at nurseries than warehouses. On average, twice as many *X. crassiusculus* were trapped with the ethanol + α-pinene lure than with ethanol. Only two of these beetles were trapped with the exotic *Ips* lure. *Xyleborinus saxeseni* (Ratzeburg) was the second most commonly intercepted scolytine beetle species, and five times more beetles were trapped at nurseries than warehouses. On average, more *X. saxeseni* were trapped with the ethanol and ethanol + α-pinene lures. Only one of these beetles was trapped with the exotic *Ips* lure. *Cnestus mutilatus* (Blandford) was the third most commonly intercepted species. This beetle was only trapped at nurseries and was never trapped with the exotic *Ips* lure. About twice as many were trapped with ethanol than ethanol + α-pinene.

THE FUTURE OF GREEN ASH BEHIND, WITHIN, AND AHEAD OF THE ADVANCING FRONT OF EMERALD ASH BORER

Stephen J. Burr[1] and Deborah G. McCullough[1,2]

[1]Michigan State University, Department of Entomology, East Lansing, MI 48824
[2]Michigan State University, Department of Forestry, East Lansing, MI 48824

ABSTRACT

Emerald ash borer (EAB), *Agrilus planipennis* Fairmaire (Coleoptera: Buprestidae), is a phloem-feeding beetle native to Asia. First discovered in Detroit, Michigan and Windsor, Ontario in 2002, dendrochronological studies indicated EAB first became established in North America at least 6 to 10 years earlier in the metro Detroit area. Since its arrival, EAB has attacked native ash (*Fraxinus spp.*) trees in forest, rural, and urban settings. As ash resources are depleted, beetle populations disperse and colonize new areas. The resulting infestation wave appears to expand in all directions.

Questions consistently arise as to the status of EAB populations and the persistence of ash in forested settings, particularly in the original core of the EAB infestation in southeast Michigan. In 2010 and 2011, we sampled EAB populations and canopy ash in 24 green ash (*Fraxinus pennsylvanica*) sites, each 1 ha in size. Eight sites were located in each of three areas of southern Michigan representing (1) the original EAB Core in the southeast; (2) the Crest in mid-Michigan where EAB populations are currently peaking; and (3) the Cusp of the invasion in southwest Michigan where EAB has recently become established.

Adult beetles were captured using a variety of trapping techniques. We placed two purple double-decker panel traps coated in Pestick™ and baited with cis-3-hexenol and either an 80:20 mix of Manuka and Phoebe oil (2010) or Manuka oil only (2011). Three uninfested green ash nursery trees (2-3 cm diameter) were planted in each site. Two naturally regenerated ash trees in each site were girdled (1 m high; 15 cm wide) to elicit a chemical stress response that attracts EAB. Two untreated control trees of similar size in each site were also chosen. A sticky band consisting of a 30 cm wide band of plastic wrap coated in Tanglefoot® was wrapped around each planted, girdled, and control tree (1.5 m high). Beetles were collected at 2 week intervals and returned to campus to check identification. Larval density was determined in fall by felling all planted, girdled, and control trees, debarking alternate sections to count galleries.

Overstory ash trees (diameter at breast height (d.b.h.)≥10 cm) were counted along two belt transects running diagonally across sites in an X-formation. Sites were also divided into four quadrats, and overstory ash (live and dead) were counted and d.b.h. was measured in one macro plot per quadrat. Canopy dieback (EAB-related) of ash was assessed in the belt transects and macro plots.

At the center of each macro plot, green ash saplings (<3 cm in stem diameter and >18 cm tall) were counted and recorded in subplots (7 m radius). Annual sapling growth (between leaf scars) was measured using a stratified sampling system.

Results showed EAB populations persisted in Core sites although adult and larval densities were low in both 2010 and 2011. Captures of adult EAB and larval density were highest in the Crest sites in central Michigan. Populations of EAB were building in Cusp sites, where adult captures nearly doubled from 2010 to 2011. As expected, overstory ash mortality was highest in the Core, lowest in the Cusp, and increasing in Crest sites where EAB density is peaking. Live ash basal area was highest in Cusp sites and lowest in the Core. Dead ash basal area was highest in the Core but increased 7-fold in Cusp sites from 2010 to 2011. While overstory ash persisted in some Core sites, canopy condition of most ash was generally poor. In the Crest, overstory ash continued to decline, and dieback increased in most sites from 2010 to 2011. In Cusp sites, trees showed little to no signs of infestation in 2010, but dieback is increasing as the EAB populations build. Ash sapling densities were lower in Cusp sites compared to sites where ash populations have been highly impacted by EAB.

AN ILLUSTRATED GUIDE TO THE LARVA OF
AGRILUS PLANIPENNIS FAIRMAIRE (EMERALD ASH BORER)
(COLEOPTERA: BUPRESTIDAE)

M. Lourdes Chamorro[1], Mark G. Volkovitsh[2], Robert A. Haack[3],
Therese M. Poland[3], and Steven W. Lingafelter[1]

[1]USDA Agricultural Research Service, c/o National Museum of Natural History, Washington, DC 20560
[2]Zoological Institute, Russian Academy of Sciences, RU-199034 St. Petersburg, Russia
[3]U.S. Forest Service, Northern Research Station, East Lansing, MI 48823

ABSTRACT

We provide the most detailed description of the immature stages of *Agrilus planipennis* Fairmaire to date and illustrate suites of larval characters useful in distinguishing among *Agrilus* Curtis species and instars. Immature stages of eight species of *Agrilus* were examined and imaged using light and scanning electron microscopy. Details of these features are presented. For *A. planipennis,* all preimaginal stages (egg, instars I-IV, prepupa, and pupa) were described. A combination of 14 character states were identified that serve to distinguish larvae of *A. planipennis*. Our results support the segregation of *Agrilus* larvae into two sets: the *A. viridis* and *A. ater* assemblages, with *A. planipennis* being more similar to the former. Additional evidence is provided in favor of excluding *A. planipennis* from the subgenus *Uragrilus*.

MINOR COMPONENTS OF THE MALE-PRODUCED
SIREX NOCTILIO PHEROMONE, A BLEND
THAT ATTRACTS BOTH SEXES

Miriam Cooperband[1], Ashley Hartness[1], Tappey Jones[2],
Kelley Zylstra[3], and Victor C. Mastro[1]

[1]USDA APHIS, PPQ, CPHST, Buzzards Bay, MA 02542
[2]Virginia Military Institute, Department of Chemistry, Lexington, VA 24450
[3]USDA APHIS, PPQ, CPHST, Syracuse, NY 13212

ABSTRACT

The European woodwasp, *Sirex noctilio* F., oviposits into pine trees depositing a phytotoxic mucus and a pathogenic fungus which together can kill the tree. Native to Eurasia, is has become a serious pest of pine trees in many regions around the world where it has been introduced. Chemical ecology research on this species has mostly focused on host odors, whereas research on mate finding has been limited. Previous work found that males more than 1 d old attracted other males in a Y-tube olfactometer and produced a large amount of (*Z*)-3-decenol, but that compound alone was not found to be attractive. This research aimed to identify minor compounds that could be added to the major compound to make an attractive synthetic pheromone blend.

New efforts were focused on finding and characterizing minor pheromone components. Volatiles were collected from males for use in gas chromatography coupled with electroantennographic detection (GC-EAD), using male antennae to look for minor components that elicited antennal responses. Based on the GC-EAD responses to natural male odors, a number of small peaks that produced antennal responses were examined using gas chromatography mass spectrometry (GC-MS), to compile a tentative list of potential identifications of minor compounds. Those compounds were acquired in synthetic form and tested for antennal responses and similarity in retention time to the natural compounds. Synthetic compounds that elicited strong antennal responses were then tested in various concentrations and blends in the Y-tube olfactometer using males. After testing 26 combinations of compounds and concentrations, we found that a 100:1 blend of the main component with (Z)-4-decenol and a 100:1:1 blend of the main component with (Z)-4-decenol and (*E,E*)-2,4-decadienal, elicited male attraction in the Y-tube. A wind tunnel was used to test attraction of both sexes to the two blends. Both males and females were attracted to the synthetic 3-compound blend at 100:1:1 of (*Z*)-3-decenol, (*Z*)-4-decenol, and (*E,E*)-2,4-decadienal.

COLOR PREFERENCES OF *SPATHIUS AGRILI*, A PARASITOID OF EMERALD ASH BORER

Miriam Cooperband[1], Allard Cossé[2], Ashley Hartness[1], and Victor C. Mastro[1]

[1]USDA APHIS, PPQ, CPHST, Buzzards Bay, MA 02542
[2]USDA ARS, National Center for Agricultural Utilization Research, Peoria, IL 61604

ABSTRACT

Spathius agrili Yang (Hymenoptera: Braconidae), native to China, has been released in North America as a biological control agent against the emerald ash borer (EAB), *Agrilus planipennis* Fairmaire (Coleoptera: Buprestidae). Techniques to evaluate whether or not this species has established are limited because there are no effective ways to trap this species. In order to sample for *S. agrili,* trees need to be felled and logs peeled or reared out in search of the developing parasitoids, which then need to be identified to distinguish them from native species in the same genus. Since the discovery of a seven-component, male-produced pheromone for *S. agrili* (Cossé et al, submitted), species-specific trapping may provide a more feasible approach for evaluating the establishment of this species in North America.

A laminar flow, push-pull wind tunnel was used to test attraction and landing of *S. agrili* to a pheromone-baited disc with halves of different colors. Six colors (red, black, white, green, yellow, and purple) were tested against each other in pairs to determine if color affected landing behavior. The green and purple were similar in color (wavelength spectrum and reflectance), but not an exact match to the colors used for EAB field traps. Female virgins were released in the downwind end of the wind tunnel, and the number of wasps that flew upwind and landed on each choice was recorded. Data were examined using chi-square test ($P=0.05$).

Flight response rates of female, virgin *S. agrili* ranged from 61.4 percent (black vs. purple) to 97.7 percent (white vs. green). Landing response rates ranged from 39.6 percent (purple vs. yellow) to 81.5 percent (green vs. black). Yellow, green, and white sides were landed upon preferentially to black, red, or purple. Yellow was preferred over red or black; white was preferred over red or purple; and green was preferred over yellow or black. An improved understanding of the color preferences displayed by *S. agrili* when landing on surfaces may facilitate the designing of a pheromone-baited trap for this species.

A COMPARISON OF ELECTROPHYSIOLOGICALLY DETERMINED SPECTRAL RESPONSES IN SEVEN SUBSPECIES OF *LYMANTRIA*

Damon J. Crook, E. Hibbard, and Victor C. Mastro

USDA APHIS, PPQ, CPHST, Buzzards Bay, MA 02542

The gypsy moth (*Lymantria dispar* Linnaeus) is one of the most recognized and devastating pests of forests in the United States. It is known to feed on more than 500 species of plants, primarily broad leafed trees and ornamental shrubs, especially oaks. Each year, approximately $11 million is spent on gypsy moth control. The Asian varieties of gypsy moth known as Asian gypsy moth (AGM) pose an even greater risk because, unlike the European variety, AGM females are active fliers (up to 20 miles).

The Asian gypsy moth is defined by the United States Department of Agriculture as "any biotype of *Lymantria dispar* (sensu lato) possessing female flight capability". Since 1991, there have been repeated incursions into North America by AGM. These incursions resulted mainly because gravid females are attracted to lights at Russian ports. They then deposit eggs on cargo and ships which head to North American ports. The moth *Lymantria mathura* Moore, known as the pink moth (and rosy Russian gypsy moth) is a native polyphagous defoliator of orchards and hardwood forests in Russia, China, Japan, and India. Its wide host range and distribution in temperate forests from the Russian Far East to Japan suggests it could establish in North America should it be accidentally introduced. Females are readily attracted to artificial lights, and like AGM, are capable of depositing egg masses on Russian ships and containers bound for North America.

Studying the visual capabilities of *Lymantria* spp. may help us to better understand their attraction to the lighting in ports and on ships. The simplest way to determine the spectral responses of a visual receptor system is to record the combined responses of several receptors, the electroretinogram (ERG). This information allows one to delimit the detectable range of colors to the insect being studied and leads to the possible evaluation of stimuli that might evoke a behavioral response. The aim of this paper was to survey the spectral responsiveness of several *Lymantria* species using electrophysiological methods (ERG) developed by Crook et al (2009) and compare the results with reported behavioral responses.

We tested the following moth subspecies from our Otis lab-reared colonies:

Japanese - Northern Iwate district (JGM) - *Lymantria dispar japonica*
Chinese - Tianjin (AGM) - *Lymantria dispar asiatica.*
Korean - Pyeon Chang (AGM) - *Lymantria dispar asiatica*
Eastern Russia - Inland Dalnerechensk (AGM) - *Lymantria dispar asiatica*
Eastern Russia - Primorsky Port region (AGM) - *Lymantria dispar asiatica*
North American - Otis NJSS strain (NAGM) - *Lymantria dispar dispar*
Russian Rosy 'Gypsy' Moth - (RGM) - *Lymantria mathura*

Two ERG runs were done for each moth. The first ERG run involved stimulating the insect with wavelengths between 300 and 700 nm in increments of 20 nm (presented randomly). A reference wavelength of

360 nm was flashed onto the moth preparation every four stimulations so that data could be normalized against it. The second ERG run stimulated the insect with wavelengths between 300 nm and 420 nm in increments of 5 nm. For the second ERG runs, reference wavelengths of 600 nm were flashed onto the moth after four random stimulations. Males and females were tested in both sets of ERG runs.

A small peak in sensitivity was seen in the UV region at around 360 nm for all the moths and sexes tested. A larger second peak in sensitivity was seen at around 500 nm (blue-green region). No distinct response to red was found. All sub species showed a similar trend in their visual capabilities. There were no obvious differences between male and female responses for each sub species tested. This supports retinogram data taken for *L. dispar* in a study by Brown and Cameron (1977).

When all moth sub species (except *L. mathura*) were screened between 300-420 nm (in 5 nm increments), we found responses to plateau at around 360 nm. Ports should try to avoid using lighting systems or bulbs that have a UV output of around 360 nm.

Literature Cited

Brown, E.A.; Cameron, A.E. 1977. **Studies of the compound eye of *Lymantria dispar* (Lepidoptera: Lymantriidae) males, and behavioral implications.** Canadian Entomologist. 109: 255-260.

Crook, D.J.; Francese, J.A.; Zylstra, K.E.; Fraser, I.; Sawyer, A.J.; Bartels, D.W.; Lance, D.R.; Mastro, V.C. 2009. **Laboratory and field response of the emerald ash borer (Coleoptera: Buprestidae), to selected regions of the electromagnetic spectrum.** Journal of Economic Entomology. 102: 2160-2169.

THE LIFE CYCLE OF HEMLOCK WOOLLY ADELGID: A CASE STUDY FOR THE GRAPHICAL EXPLANATION OF DATA

Vincent D'Amico[1] and Nathan P. Havill[2]

[1]U.S. Forest Service, Northern Research Station, Newark, DE 19716
[2]U.S. Forest Service, Northern Research Station, Hamden, CT 06514

ABSTRACT

 The hemlock woolly adelgid (HWA), *Adelges tsugae*, is a major pest of hemlock (*Tsuga* spp.) in the eastern United States. This insect has been responsible for millions of dollars of damage to the two hemlock species which play a vital role in the ecology of many eastern forests. Efforts have been made by many scientists and research teams to develop methods of control, with limited success to date.

Molecular genetics have shown that the eastern U.S. population of HWA was introduced from Japan, while a separate lineage is native to western North America. The life cycles of HWA in North America and Japan are not consistent. In Japan, there are two lineages of hemlock woolly adelgid that specialize on each of the Japanese hemlock species, *T. sieboldii* and *T. diversifolia*. *Tsuga sieboldii* grows at lower elevations and further south, while *T. diversifolia* grows to the north at higher elevations. The population in the eastern United States originated from the *T. sieboldii* lineage. In Japan, this lineage has a winged form that moves from hemlock to spruce where it goes through an additional three generations, forms galls, and engages in sexual reproduction. The North American populations of HWA do not reproduce on spruce, limiting their life cycle to two generations on hemlock. In the East, winged migrants are produced that cannot reproduce on native spruce species, while in the West, HWA appears to have lost the winged form entirely.

The differences between reproduction of HWA populations on two different hosts and in different geographical regions have made a comprehensive and comprehendible illustration of its life cycle difficult. Compounding this difficulty is regional variation in generation times (e.g., between CT and VA) that does not allow life stages to be universally tied to months of the year. The general tendency for life cycle figures is to attempt a representation of life stages as a circle with months around the perimeter as a natural way to connote the "cycle" aspect. With an insect such as HWA, this conceptualization is problematic and not as fruitful as a straightforward representation of the duration and seasonality of each life stage in a linear fashion on each host, positioned so that the timing is (generally) correct for all the regions where it occurs.

Below, we present a figure for the life cycle of HWA in Japan and North America. This is intended to replace an older, less informative life cycle diagram. The image can be obtained by contacting either author, or by downloading it from forestinsects.org/HWA.

A brief guide to the HWA life cycle figure. Sets of five different color bars were used for each generation. The different colors make it easier to determine that HWA has a total of five generations on two host trees in its native range in Japan, but only two in the United States. The choice of colors was vetted by the second author, who is red-green color blind. Bars are given increasingly greater thickness to connote the increasing sizes of each life stage. The "N" labels for bars were considered necessary because HWA generations do not always have the same number of instars; thus "N1" for "first instar nymph", etc. Dashed arrowheads show the production of eggs and connect generations. A lightly colored background was used for each tree host, with white seasonal dividing lines (created by "negative space") proved less distracting than dark lines. Seasons were substituted for months because regional and latitudinal differences preclude showing precise times for HWA phenology.

For further reading:

Havill, N.; Montgomery, M.; Keena, M. 2011. **Hemlock woolly adelgid and its hemlock hosts: a global perspective**. In: Onken, B.; Reardon, R., tech. coord. Implementation and status of biological control of the hemlock woolly adelgid. FHTET-2011-04. Morgantown, WV: U.S. Department of Agriculture, Forest Service, Forest Health Technology Enterprise Team: 3-14.

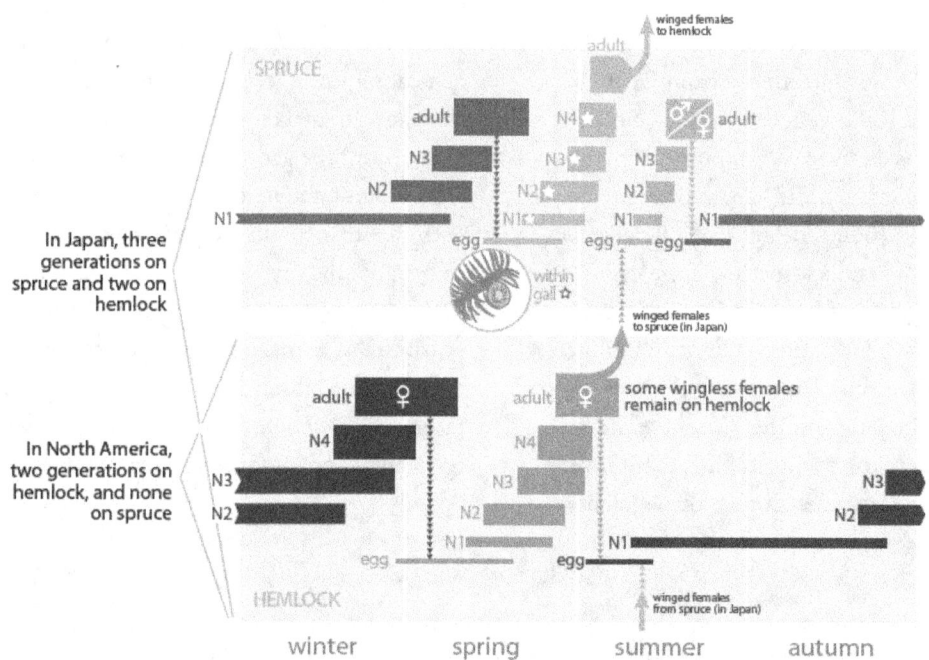

VOLUNTEER STREAM MONITORING FOR INVASIVE *PHYTOPHTHORA* SPECIES IN WESTERN WASHINGTON

Marianne Elliott, Gary A. Chastagner, Katie Coats, Annie DeBauw, and Kathy Riley

Washington State University, Puyallup Research and Extension Center, Puyallup, WA 98371

ABSTRACT

To supplement state agencies in their monitoring for *Phytophthora ramorum*, the exotic sudden oak death (SOD) pathogen, a community-based stream monitoring program was initiated in 2010 with a pilot study of six streams. In 2011, monitoring was done at 12 sites in the Puget Sound region of western Washington, expanding on the streams currently being sampled by the Washington Department of Natural Resources (WADNR) as part of the national *P. ramorum* survey and on nursery surveys by Washington State Department of Agriculture (WSDA). This project allows for early detection of *P. ramorum* and other invasive *Phytophthora* species, as well as examining the biodiversity of *Phytophthora* spp. in stream ecosystems.

Volunteers included Master Gardeners, high school, community college, and University of Washington Tacoma students, and others. Lecture and lab sessions were taught as part of the college classes to introduce students to plant pathology, *Phytophthora* diseases, and laboratory methods. High school and college students worked on group or individual projects related to *Phytophthora* in the lab at Washington State University-Puyallup. Students did independent study projects on growth of *P. ramorum* on agar made from stream water and varying nutrient concentrations, antagonism of *Trichoderma* spp. to *P. ramorum*, tested pathogenicity of some species isolated from streams on conifer seedlings, and the effectiveness of spraying shoes with disinfectants after visiting a contaminated site. In a class project, the bait in a bottle method was used at a site in Puyallup.

For bait, volunteers used *Rhododendron* spp. leaves and leaf material from various plant species found on the site. The baiting process involved placing leaves in mesh bags and deploying them in the stream for 2 weeks. After bait retrieval, the leaves were cultured on *Phytophthora*-selective media, and colonies were then transferred onto V8 agar. Species were identified using molecular and cultural methods. *P. ramorum* was found at one site in 2011 that was already known to be positive, but all other sites were negative for *P. ramorum*. Other Oomycetes, including several species of *Phytophthora*, *Pythium*, and *Saprolegnia* were also identified.

Students described this project as "eye opening and a great way to apply skills they had learned to real research within their community." This project has been very successful in raising the awareness of waterborne plant pathogens such as *P. ramorum* and the damage they cause in the community. We plan to integrate this into the STEM education program with the Puyallup School District in 2012, as well as continue to provide opportunities for local high school and college students.

THE WESTERN BARK BEETLE RESEARCH GROUP

Christopher J. Fettig[1], Barbara J. Bentz[2], Mary E. Dix[3], Nancy E. Gillette[4],
Rick G. Kelsey[5], John E. Lundquist[6], Ann M. Lynch[7], Jose F. Negrón[8],
Robert A. Progar[9], and Steven J. Seybold[1]

[1]U.S. Forest Service, Pacific Southwest Research Station, Davis, CA 95618
[2]U.S. Forest Service, Rocky Mountain Research Station, Logan, UT 84321
[3]U.S. Forest Service, Research and Development, Arlington, VA 22209
[4]U.S. Forest Service, Pacific Southwest Research Station, Albany, CA 94710
[5]U.S. Forest Service, Pacific Northwest Research Station, Corvallis, OR 97331
[6]U.S. Forest Service, Forest Health Protection and Pacific Northwest
Research Station, Anchorage, AK 99503
[7]U.S. Forest Service, Rocky Mountain Research Station, Tucson, AZ 85721
[8]U.S. Forest Service, Rocky Mountain Research Station, Fort Collins, CO 80526
[9]U.S. Forest Service, Pacific Northwest Research Station, LaGrande, OR 97850

ABSTRACT

Bark beetles cause extensive tree mortality in coniferous forests of western North America and play an important role in the disturbance ecology of these ecosystems. For many years, U.S. Forest Service research scientists (www.fs.fed.us/research/) studied the biology, ecology, and management of tree-killing bark beetles. Historically, research reflected an emphasis placed on protection of timber resources. Today, changes in societal values, global trading practices, and an increased awareness of the importance of disturbances in the functioning of forest ecosystems present previously unexplored questions. The Forest Service Western Bark Beetle Research Group (WBBRG) was created in 2007 and includes scientists from the three western Forest Service research stations with expertise in bark beetle research, development, and application in the West. This poster highlights our current research portfolio. Annual reports of research accomplishments are available at www.usu.edu/beetle/wbbrg_bark_beetle.htm.

THERMOREGULATORY BEHAVIOR AND FUNGAL INFECTION: IMPACT ON THE SURVIVAL OF THE ASIAN LONGHORNED BEETLE, *ANOPLOPHORA GLABRIPENNIS*

Joanna J. Fisher and Ann E. Hajek

Cornell University, Department of Entomology, Ithaca, NY 14853-2601

Asian longhorned beetles, *Anoplophora glabripennis* (Motschulsky), are invasive woodborers from China that have been introduced into the eastern United States and have the potential to negatively impact economic and environmental interests in U.S. hardwood and urban forests. The entomopathogenic fungus *Metarhizium brunneum* (= *M. anisopliae*) Petch is under development for control of *A. glabripennis*. However, as a result of elevating their body temperatures through basking (behavioral fever), some insect species are able to fight off or delay the impacts of pathogens. Studies of *A. glabripennis* in China yielded observations of beetles in the sun at the tops of tree canopies early in the morning. These observations suggest that *A. glabripennis* might thermoregulate, so we investigated the potential use of behavioral fever by *A. glabripennis* in response to fungal infections.

Both uninoculated and *M. brunneum*-inoculated *A. glabripennis* were placed individually into temperature gradients 2, 5, and 8 days after fungal infection to determine whether they exhibit behavioral fever and what impact temperature preference has on their longevity. Adult *A. glabripennis* inoculated with *M. brunneum* did not exhibit behavioral fever even though exhibiting behavioral fever could have significantly increased their survival. Holding *M. brunneum*-infected *A. glabripennis* at 34 °C for 5 h a day significantly increased beetle survival by 2 d compared to beetles held at lower temperatures. Beetles held at 34 °C most likely lived longer because fungal growth was negatively affected, as *M. brunneum* incubated at 34 °C for 5 h a day grew significantly slower compared to when it was incubated at lower temperatures.

Adult *A. glabripennis* behaviorally thermoregulated and maintained average body temperatures that were 3 °C above ambient. We did not, however, observe a morning basking behavior. To our knowledge, this is the first experiment addressing behavioral thermoregulation in cerambycid beetles. The results of this study suggest that a control program involving *M. brunneum* would not be negatively impacted by behavioral fevering because, although the fungus is inhibited at higher temperatures, the beetles did not elevate their temperatures enough to inhibit fungal growth.

FACTORS AFFECTING STAGE-SPECIFIC PERFORMANCE OF *TETROPIUM FUSCUM* (COLEOPTERA: CERAMBYCIDAE)

Leah Flaherty[1,2], Dan Quiring[1], Deepa Pureswaran[3], and Jon Sweeney[2]

[1] University of New Brunswick, Faculty of Forestry and Environmental Management, Fredericton, NB E3B 5A3
[2] Natural Resources Canada, Canadian Forest Service, Fredericton, NB E3B 5P7
[3] Natural Resources Canada, Canadian Forest Service, Sainte-Foy, QC G1V 4C7

ABSTRACT

In its native Europe, *Tetropium fuscum* (F.) (Coleoptera: Cerambycidae) colonizes weakened Norway spruce, *Picea abies* (L.) Karst., and is not considered a pest. In Nova Scotia, this exotic beetle can kill apparently healthy red spruce, *Picea rubens* Sarg., and has been classified as a quarantine pest by the Canadian Food Inspection Agency since 2000. Any mechanisms allowing *T. fuscum* to colonize healthier spruce trees in Canada than in Europe are unknown, but may be related to its colonization of a novel North American host and/or its new natural enemy complex. We are investigating the relative impact of these factors on *T. fuscum* performance in Canada using manipulative field experiments. Specifically, we exposed developing *T. fuscum* to different host tree species (Norway versus red spruce), tree conditions (girdled versus healthy), and levels of protection from natural enemies and competitors, and evaluated subsequent performance (stage-specific survival, mortality factors, development rate, and adult size). Survival and development rate were greater on stressed than on healthy trees, and there was no effect of exposure to natural enemies, contrary to previous results. Timing of attack was an important factor influencing all measures of performance, and total survival was highest when larvae attacked mid-season. Preliminary results indicated that survival was reduced on Norway compared to red spruce, but experiments are ongoing.

EFFICACY OF MULTI-FUNNEL TRAPS FOR CAPTURING EMERALD ASH BORER: EFFECT OF COLOR, SIZE, AND TRAP COATING

Joseph A. Francese[1], Michael L. Rietz[2], David R. Lance[1],
Ivich Fraser[2], and Victor C. Mastro[1]

[1]USDA APHIS, PPQ, CPHST, Buzzards Bay, MA 02542
[2]USDA APHIS, PPQ, CPHST, Brighton, MI 48116

ABSTRACT

Tens of thousands of adhesive-coated purple prism traps are deployed annually in the United States to survey for the invasive emerald ash borer, *Agrilus planipennis* Fairmaire (Coleoptera: Buprestidae). A reusable, more user-friendly trap is desired by program managers, surveyors, and researchers. Field assays were conducted in southeastern Michigan in 2009 and 2010 to ascertain the feasibility of using nonsticky traps as survey and detection tools for emerald ash borer. Rain-X® has been shown to increase EAB catch in funnel traps over glue-coated and untreated funnel traps (Francese et al. 2011).

The standard size multi-funnel trap we have used since 2009 is a 12-unit model. Miller and Crowe (2009) found that funnel trap length (number of funnels) played a role in capturing some species of bark- and woodboring beetles. We tested different sizes of traps (number of funnels) and found that multi-funnel trap size does play a role in capture of EAB. We tested green and purple versions of 4-unit, 8-unit, 12-unit, and 16-unit traps. All traps were coated with Rain-X®. There was no significant interaction between color and number of funnels per trap, so green and purple traps were combined for statistical analysis. Twelve-unit multi-funnel traps were more effective than other traps as they caught more beetles than the smaller traps and were not as unwieldy as the 16-unit traps. Sex ratio was not affected by number of funnels per trap.

Fluon® has been shown to increase captures of cerambycids in baited intercept panel traps over Rain-X® treated and control traps (Graham et al. 2010). While Fluon® is clear when applied to a surface, it dries white. Concerned that this could change the attractiveness of the trap to EAB, we added pigments to a Fluon® base to change the color of the liquid and the dried residue. The pigments had previously been used to create the green and purple funnel trap plastic color. The addition of the green pigment to Fluon® was unnecessary since nontinted (white) Fluon® applied to green plastic funnel traps produced the highest catch of all trap treatments. There was no significant difference among Rain-X® and Fluon® treated purple multi-funnel traps and green-tinted Fluon® treated traps. Treating the traps was necessary because uncoated traps were out-caught by Fluon® and Rain-X® coated traps, regardless of color.

Literature Cited

Francese, J.A.; Fraser, I.; Lance, D.R.; Mastro, V.C. 2011. **Efficacy of multifunnel traps for capturing emerald ash borer (Coleoptera: Buprestidae): effect of color, glue, and other trap coatings.** Journal of Economic Entomology. 104(3): 1235-1241.

Graham, E.E.; Mitchell, R.F.; Reagel, P.F.; Barbour, J. D.; Millar, J.G.; Hanks, L.M. 2010. **Treating panel traps with a flouropolymer enhances their efficiency in capturing cerambycid beetles.** Journal of Economic Entomology. 103 (3): 641-647.

Miller, D.R.; Crowe C.M. 2009. **Length of multiple-funnel traps affects catches of some bark and wood boring beetles in a slash pine stand in northern Florida.** Florida Entomologist. 92 (3): 506-507.

IMPROVING DETECTION TOOLS FOR EMERALD ASH BORER: COMPARISON OF PRISM AND MULTI-FUNNEL TRAPS AT HIGH AND LOW POPULATION DENSITY SITES

Joseph A. Francese[1], Michael L. Rietz[2], Damon J. Crook[1], David R. Lance[1], Ivich Fraser[2], and Victor C. Mastro[1]

[1]USDA APHIS, PPQ, CPHST, Buzzards Bay, MA 02542
[2]USDA APHIS, PPQ, CPHST, Brighton, MI 48116

ABSTRACT

The emerald ash borer (EAB), *Agrilus planipennis* Fairmaire, survey trap currently used in the United States is a prism trap constructed from a stock purple corrugated plastic. Recent electroretinogram assays have demonstrated that male and female EAB are sensitive to light in the UV, violet, and green (420–430, 460, and 530–560 nm, respectively) ranges of the visible spectrum, while mated females are also sensitive to light in the red (640–670 nm) range (Crook et al. 2009). Trapping studies have shown that green traps painted in the mid-range (22-67 percent) of reflectance (brightness) and purple traps painted with a color originally shown to be attractive to buprestids were most attractive to EAB (Francese et al. 2010). Several plastics have been produced from these colors, and our goal was to determine if these plastics can improve on and serve as a new alternative to plastics already in use for EAB surveys. In 2010, six colors were tested at 5-8 m in the lower canopy of heavily infested ash woodlots:

1. Coroplast® purple plastic–the standard color used for EAB surveys in the United States since 2008.

2. TSU purple paint–a color found by Oliver et al. (2002) to be attractive to at least 31 species of buprestids including some *Agrilus* spp.; painted on translucent plastic prism traps.

3. SABIC® purple plastic–a newly manufactured plastic based on the TSU purple paint.

4. Coroplast® green plastic–based on a paint described by Crook et al. (2009) as being attractive to EAB; 540 nm, 67 percent reflectance; sometimes referred to as light green.

5. New green paint–found by Francese et al. (2010) to also be attractive to EAB; 530 nm, 49 percent reflectance; sometimes referred to as medium or dark green.

6. SABIC® Green plastic–a newly manufactured plastic based on the new green paint.

In 2011, treatments 1, 3, 4, and 6 were tested along with two other colors:

- Vidmar purple plastic–a purple plastic based on TSU purple, manufactured by a different company than Sabic.

- Purple card stock–a wax-coated card stock prism designed to be more user-friendly; folds to a small size and is lighter than corrugated plastic.

New purple and green plastic traps showed promise as alternatives to the standard purple corrugated plastic, but there was a greater degree of variability in catch on green traps than on purple traps in 2010 and among all traps in 2011. Several of the purple card stock traps fell apart during the field season, so these need work if they are to be an alternative to the current corrugated plastic.

Results from studies performed in heavily infested sites may not always match up with what is found along the edges of the infestation. Marshall et al. (2010) found that purple prism traps, while yielding lower catches than green traps in Michigan, had a higher detection rate (caught at least one beetle) in outlier infestations. The detection tools/outlier study this year was conducted on public land along or near the leading edges of the current emerald ash borer infestation in nine states: Indiana, Kentucky, Maryland, Minnesota, Missouri, New York, Pennsylvania, West Virginia, and Wisconsin. Four trap designs were tested:

- Standard purple prism
- SABIC® purple prism
- SABIC® green prism
- Green (12-unit) multi-funnel treated with Rain-X®

Prism traps were coated with Tangle-Trap®. All four designs were baited with a Manuka oil (50mg/d)/*cis*-3-hexenol (50mg/d) lure. Traps were placed at least 30 m apart from each other within replicates, and replicates were placed at least 800 m from each other within states. Ninety-nine replicates were placed among the nine states. Of the 99 reps, 5 were lost to Mississippi River flooding in Missouri and 17 did not catch a single beetle (no detection). For the analyses, only the 77 replicates that recorded at least one beetle were used. Marshall et al. (2009) defined low and high density sites based on visual signs and symptoms observed on trees. They saw a natural break in trap catch between low (≤ 87) and high (≥ 273) density sites. We used these same numbers to define low (n=56) and high (n=7) density sites, and defined the 14 sites where trap catch fell between these numbers as medium density sites.

Trap catch was highest on Sabic purple prism traps, and there was no significant difference between trap catch among the other trap types. The proportion of detection was highest on Sabic purple prism traps among total sites. It was also highest at low density sites. There were no significant differences among any of the other trap types. In replicates where only a single trap recorded a detection and the other three trap types did not, the SABIC® purple prism, Standard purple prism, SABIC® green prism, and green multi-funnel were responsible for 10, 2, 2, and 1 detections, respectively.

Literature Cited

Crook, D.J.; Francese, J.A.; Zylstra, K.E.; Fraser, I.; Sawyer, A.J., Bartels, D.W.; Lance, D.R.; Mastro, V.C. 2009. **Laboratory and field response of the emerald ash borer, *Agrilus planipennis* (Coleoptera: Buprestidae), to selected regions of the electromagnetic spectrum.** Journal of Economic Entomology. 102: 2160–2169.

Francese, J.A.; Crook, D.J.; Fraser, I.; Lance, D. R.; Sawyer, A.J.; Mastro, V.C. 2010. **Optimization of trap color for emerald ash borer (Coleoptera: Buprestidae).** Journal of Economic Entomology. 103(4): 1235-1241.

Marshall, J.M.; Storer, A.J.; Fraser, I.; Beachy, J.A.; Mastro, V.C. 2009. **Effectiveness of differing trap types for the detection of emerald ash borer (Coleoptera: Buprestidae).** Environmental Entomology. 38: 1226-1234.

Marshall, J.M.; Storer, A.J.; Fraser, I.; Mastro, V.C. 2010. **Efficacy of trap and lure types for detection of *Agrilus planipennis* (Col., Buprestidae) at low density.** Journal of Applied Entomology. 134: 296-302.

Oliver, J.B.; Youssef, N.; Fare, D.; Halcomb, M.; Scholl, S.; Klingeman, W.; Flanagan, P. 2002. **Monitoring buprestid borers in production nursery areas.** In: Haun, G., ed. Proceedings of the 29th annual meeting of the Tennessee Entomological Society; 2002 October 10-11; Nashville, TN: 17-23.

DISTRIBUTION AND SYMPTOMS OF THOUSAND CANKERS DISEASE ON BLACK WALNUT IN TENNESSEE

Jerome F. Grant[1], Mark T. Windham[1], Gregory J. Wiggins[1], Paris L. Lambdin[1], and Walker Haun[2]

[1] The University of Tennessee, Department of Entomology and Plant Pathology, Knoxville, TN 37996
[2] Tennessee Department of Agriculture, Division of Regulatory Services, Nashville, TN 37204

ABSTRACT

Black walnut, *Juglans nigra* L., is native to the eastern and midwestern United States, where it is an important timber commodity as well as an economically important specialty crop species, highly valued for its wood, nut production, and as a nursery plant. Although it is not native to the western United States, black walnut has been transplanted and is grown throughout urban areas. The black walnut industry is now threatened by a new insect/fungal disease complex which has invaded the native range of black walnut and has tremendous potential to cause immediate problems.

Large numbers of black walnut trees in the western United States have died over the last decade. Researchers concluded that this mortality was caused by a new disease complex called thousand cankers disease (TCD), which involves the fungus *Geosmithia morbida* (Ascomycota: Hypocreales) vectored by walnut twig beetle, *Pityophthorus juglandis*, and represents the first documentation of *G. morbida* as a pathogen of black walnut. This beetle is native to the western United States where it is found in several states.

The discovery in July 2010 of TCD on black walnut in its native range in eastern Tennessee represented the first documentation of this disease complex east of Colorado. In 2011, TCD was found in Pennsylvania and Virginia. The impact of TCD on black walnut in its native range is unclear; however, scientists speculate that this disease, if left unmanaged, could cause the extinction of this important tree species in its native range. This paper provides an update on TCD in Tennessee.

During the last 2 years, the Tennessee Department of Agriculture and the Tennessee Division of Forestry conducted surveys to determine the extent of TCD in counties in eastern Tennessee. Samples of symptomatic black walnuts were sent to the University of Tennessee for processing. The causative agents, walnut twig beetle and *G. morbida*, were documented in six counties. Tree mortality was observed in two counties, and tree decline, which may be attributed to previous droughts or TCD, was observed in numerous counties. The TCD-documented counties (four in 2010 and two in 2011) were quarantined by the Tennessee Department of Agriculture, and an additional 10 buffer counties were also regulated. Several symptoms including yellowing and dieback were closely associated with TCD incidence. Several signs (entrance/exit holes, beetle galleries, and inner cankers) also were highly correlated with the presence of beetles and/or *G. morbida*, but their presence was difficult to determine in the field.

The presence of TCD in Tennessee provides a tremendous opportunity to expand research and outreach activities to better understand this disease and its causative agent in the native range of black walnut in the eastern United States. Knowledge gained here can be applied throughout the native range of black walnut to enable scientists to develop better management strategies to limit the impact of this potentially devastating disease.

COMPARATIVE ASSESSMENT OF MORTALITY OF EASTERN HEMLOCK IN BIOLOGICALLY-TREATED AREAS USING SPATIAL ANALYSES

Abdul Hakeem[1], Jerome F. Grant[1], Gregory J. Wiggins[1], Rusty Rhea[2], Paris L. Lambdin[1], David S. Buckley[3], Frank A. Hale[4], and Thomas Colson[5]

[1] The University of Tennessee, Department of Entomology and Plant Pathology, Knoxville, TN 37996
[2] U.S. Forest Service, Forest Health Protection, Asheville, NC 28804
[3] The University of Tennessee, Department of Forestry, Wildlife, and Fisheries, Knoxville, TN 37996
[4] The University of Tennessee, Soil, Plant and Pest Center, Nashville, TN 37211
[5] Great Smoky Mountains National Park, Gatlinburg, TN 37738

ABSTRACT

Geographic Information Systems (GIS) have been used to model the spread of pest species in various systems. Hemlock woolly adelgid, *Adelges tsugae*, was first reported on eastern hemlock, *Tsuga canadensis* (L.) Carr., in the Great Smoky Mountains National Park in 2002. This minute insect pest has caused mortality of tens of thousands of hemlock trees in the Park. To assess tree mortality, remotely-sensed digital ortho images from recovery, non-recovery, and control (no release) sites were evaluated, and percent tree mortality was compared using spatial analyses. Remotely-sensed digital ortho images (four-band color infrared, 1m-pixel resolution) were used in this study. Dead hemlocks identified by spatial analysis were supported by on-site examinations as part of another ongoing study. Additionally, on-site evaluation of tree health characteristics found that hemlock trees in recovery sites were healthier and had denser canopies than trees in non-recovery sites. This study provided useful information on how spatial analysis, coupled with on-site evaluations, can characterize hemlock mortality on a landscape scale, which may ultimately help to assess effectiveness of introduced natural enemies in forest systems. The spatial analyst tool could be used to detect outbreaks of pests and assess effectiveness of other natural enemies in forest systems. If properly developed, this spatial model will help land managers to detect dead and/or declining trees in landscapes at an early stage and to determine the extent of pest and disease outbreaks. This type of model also can assist land managers in devising appropriate management strategies, which may provide a means to maintain hemlock in natural areas.

EFFECTS OF LOG MOISTURE CONTENT ON OVIPOSITION BEHAVIOR OF *SIREX NIGRICORNIS* F. (HYMENOPTERA:SIRICIDAE)

Jessica A. Hartshorn and Fred M. Stephen

University of Arkansas, Department of Entomology, Fayetteville, AR 72701

ABSTRACT

Sirex noctilio F. (Hymenoptera: Siricidae) is an invasive woodwasp discovered in New York in 2005. With the multi-billion dollar timber industry in the southeastern United States, it is imperative that we learn more about our native woodwasps to prepare for the possible establishment of this exotic species. To do this, we recorded oviposition behavior of the native Arkansas woodwasp, *S. nigricornis* F., alone and also in the presence of a known competitor and predator, *Monochamus titillator* F. (Coleoptera: Cerambycidae). We exposed siricid females to bolts (logs; 0.75 m) to allow for oviposition by the female until death. Bolts were then removed and examined for the presence of drill holes using a dissecting microscope. This was performed for bolts with no sign of infestation by *M. titillator* and for bolts with oviposition pits by the beetle. Variance to mean ratio was calculated for each group of bolts and compared. Ratios did not differ between treatment and control bolts, however, a general avoidance of *Monochamus* bolts was observed. In addition, we felled 20 bolts and assigned treatments randomly to groups of five, resulting in four treatments (0, 15, 30, and 45 days left in the field). Cookies (3-4 cm cross-sections) were cut from the bottom, top, and center of each bolt at the end of treatment to determine wood moisture loss. Once averages for each interval were determined, it was clear that at 30 days, wood moisture content leveled off and did not drop significantly after that. Because of this, siricids were only exposed to three bolts of differing moisture content: 0, 15, and 30 days. Percent holes per bolt were then calculated, and we found that siricids prefer to oviposit in the newest bolts (0 days). These data suggest that, while the presence of *M. titillator* may inhibit the oviposition of woodwasps, females tend to prefer the most recently felled bolts.

OPERATION ADELGIFICATION: EVALUATING A RAIN DOWN TECHNIQUE TO ARTIFICIALLY INFEST SEEDLINGS WITH THE HEMLOCK WOOLLY ADELGID

Robert M. Jetton[1], Albert E. Mayfield III[2], Zaidee L. Powers[1], and Fred P. Hain[3]

[1]Camcore, North Carolina State University, Department of Forestry & Environmental Resources, Raleigh, NC 27695
[2]U.S. Forest Service, Southern Research Station, Asheville, NC 28804
[3]North Carolina State University, Department of Entomology, Raleigh, NC 27695

ABSTRACT

Over the last two decades, the hemlock woolly adelgid (HWA), *Adelges tsugae* Annand, has caused widespread decline and mortality among populations of eastern (*Tsuga canadensis* [L.] Carrière) and Carolina (*Tsuga caroliniana* Engelmann) hemlock throughout the mid-Atlantic and Southern Appalachian regions of the United States. Development of artificial infestation techniques that is efficient and reliable for screening large numbers of putatively HWA-resistant hemlock genotypes has been identified as a key research priority by the U.S. Forest Service Working Group on Genetics and Host Resistance in Hemlock. The objective of this pilot study was to determine whether a suspended branch technique (in which HWA crawlers "rain down") can adequately infest hemlock seedlings. In March 2011, eastern hemlock branches 40 cm long and heavily infested with HWA sistens adults (mean=217 ovisacs per branch) were placed bottom-side-down on 1 m cubic PVC frames with poultry wire tops. Four frames received a low ovisac treatment (24 branches) and four received a high ovisac treatment (48 branches). Branches were suspended for 3 weeks over a gridded sticky sheet (used to estimate crawler density), a Carolina hemlock seedling, and an eastern hemlock seedling. The high ovisac treatment resulted in significantly more progrediens crawlers raining down than the low ovisac treatment. Extrapolating from mean counts made on subsampled sticky sheets grids, an estimated 290,000 and 514,000 crawlers per m^2 fell beneath the low and high ovisac treatments, respectively. The number of settled progrediens adults and sistens nymphs of the subsequent generation did not differ significantly between the low and high ovisac density treatments on either Carolina or eastern hemlock. Mean settled sistens densities on test seedlings ranged between 58 and 85 nymphs per 10 cm branch. This rain down technique shows promise for applying ample infestation pressure on large numbers of seedlings simultaneously in resistance screening trials. Current and future work will compare infestation success on seedlings subject to the rain down technique versus other methods of adelgification.

AN ARTIFICIAL DIET THAT DOES NOT CONTAIN HOST MATERIAL FOR REARING THE EMERALD ASH BORER (*AGRILUS PLANIPENNIS*) LARVAE

Melody A. Keena[1], Pierluigi Bonello[2], and Hannah Nadel[3]

[1]U.S. Forest Service, Northern Research Station, Hamden, CT 06514-1703
[2]Ohio State University, Department of Plant Pathology, Columbus, OH 43214
[3]USDA APHIS, PPQ, CPHST, Buzzards Bay, MA 02542

ABSTRACT

The emerald ash borer (EAB), *Agrilus planipennis*, is a nonnative insect from Asia that threatens ash (*Fraxinus* spp.) trees in urban and natural forests of North America. Rearing larvae for research and parasitoid production currently relies heavily on host plant material. The goal of our research was to develop an artificial diet that does not contain ash phloem. To accomplish this, we evaluated the survival and development of 50-100 EAB larvae reared on several artificial diets lacking host material. Diet pieces (3-6 mm thick) were placed in tight-fitting Petri dishes (50 x 9 mm). Larvae/eggs were inserted and held at 25 °C, 65 percent relative humidity (RH), and 16h:8h (light:dark) cycle. An earlier formulation of our artificial EAB diet was modified based on analysis of the nutritional traits of phloem samples from three North American ash species (*F. americana* L., *F. pennsylvanica* Marsh, and *F. nigra* Marsh) and an EAB-resistant species from northeastern Asia (*F. mandshurica* Rupr.). Using the analysis results and larval behavior as clues to changes that might be necessary in the diet or holding methods, we now have a diet (the 34th host plant-free formulation we evaluated) and method that allows larvae to burrow in, survive (about 70 percent to pupation), and complete their development. Several modifications were needed to reach this level of survival and development: a) reducing the antimicrobial components in the diet to the lowest, functional level; b) changing protein sources in the diet from wheat germ, brewer's yeast, and casein to soy flour and casein; c) reducing diet moisture content from 60 percent to 50 percent; d) changing orientation of the dishes from horizontal to vertical; and e) not disturbing the larvae (no diet change) until they have reached the desired size. Future research will include improving pupal holding methods, assessing parasitoid acceptance of larvae reared on an artificial diet without host material, evaluating methods to rear more than one larva per container, determining phenology of EAB growth on the artificial diet, and testing allelochemicals of ash origin in other studies aiming to understand mechanisms of ash resistance to EAB.

THE FIDELITY OF FUNGAL SYMBIONTS ASSOCIATED WITH SIREX WOODWASPS IN EASTERN NORTH AMERICA

Ryan M. Kepler, Charlotte Nielsen, and Ann E. Hajek

Cornell University, Department of Entomology, Ithaca, NY 14853-2601

ABSTRACT

Woodwasps in the genus *Sirex* infest coniferous trees and engage in obligate exosymbioses with several species of *Amylostereum*, a homobasidiomycete genus of white rot fungi. Fungal spores are carried from trees by emergent females in specialized structures called mycangia, allowing vertical transmission of fungi to the next generation. Three species of *Sirex* are native to northeastern North America, and interest in the fungal associations of North American *Sirex* spp. has increased following the first North American collection of invasive *Sirex noctilio* (associated with *Amylostereum areolatum*) in New York State in 2004. This species has been known to cause widespread damage where it has been accidentally introduced to pine plantations in the Southern Hemisphere. It has been assumed that relationships between *Sirex* woodwasps and their *Amylostereum* symbionts are species specific. *Amylostereum chailletii* is the only fungus believed to be associated with North American *Sirex* woodwasps. However, isolates of *A. areolatum* with a genotype unique to North America were found in mycangia of two *S.* sp. '*nitidis*' individuals collected outside of the range of *S. noctilio*, suggesting *A. areolatum* was present prior to the introduction of *S. noctilio*. The intergenic spacer (IGS) region of nuclear ribosomal RNA has been shown to distinguish between *Amylostereum* species. This locus occurs as multiple divergent copies in *A. areolatum*, a feature that has been used to assess population structure. In this study, we employed molecular methods to examine fungal associations of *Sirex* woodwasps in eastern North America.

We successfully determined the identity of fungi present in mycangia from 192 wasps. Two of the three native *Sirex* species, *S. nigricornis* and *S.* sp. '*nitidus*', carried either *A. chailletii* or *A. areolatum*, although only one *Amylostereum* species was present per *Sirex* female. For females of the pine-preferring native *S. nigricornis*, *A. chailletii* was more commonly carried (Fisher's exact test; $P < 0.0001$) while for the spruce-preferring native, *Sirex* sp. '*nitidus*', too few individuals were collected to assess preference. All individuals of the native *S. cyaneus* carried *A. chailletii*, and *S. noctilio* always carried *A. areolatum*.

We developed a fragment analysis protocol able to resolve between the multiple copies found in *A. areolatum* that was based on size differences resulting from insertion-deletion events. No more than two IGS types were observed for *Amylostereum* strains isolated from one *Sirex* female. Only the IGS BE genotype of *A. areolatum* was recovered in native *Sirex*, regardless of whether they were collected from areas where *S. noctilio* was present or whether they emerged from the same wood as *S. noctilio*. *Sirex noctilio* carried only *A. areolatum* of the BD and D IGS genotypes, regardless of sympatry with native *Sirex*.

Our studies have demonstrated that associations between *Sirex* and *Amylostereum* can be semispecific. The propensity of *Sirex* species to actively demonstrate preferences for different *Amylostereum* species remains to be determined. As invasive *S. noctilio* increase and spread, the limits of specificity for symbiont associations among *Sirex* woodwasps will continue to be tested.

A PROBABILISTIC PATHWAY MODEL OF FOREST INSECT DISPERSAL VIA RECREATIONAL FIREWOOD TRANSPORT

Frank H. Koch[1], Denys Yemshanov[2], Roger D. Magarey[3], and William D. Smith[1]

[1]U.S. Forest Service, Southern Research Station, Research Triangle Park, NC 27709
[2]Natural Resources Canada, Canadian Forest Service, Sault Ste. Marie, ON, P6A 2E5
[3]USDA APHIS, PPQ, CPHST, Raleigh, NC 27606

ABSTRACT

Because human-mediated dispersal of invasive species is typically vector-based (e.g., via transportation corridors), spatio-temporal models that omit such vectors may poorly predict long-distance dispersal events. This issue is critical in modeling the spread of invasive forest insects by means such as recreational firewood transport, where long-distance dispersal is rare but may lead to significant impacts. This study used data from the U.S. National Recreation Reservation Service (NRRS) documenting >7 million visitor reservations at >2500 campgrounds and recreational facilities nationwide. The distribution of visitors' travel distances to these facilities is strongly leptokurtic but well fit to theoretical distributions such as the lognormal. Importantly, the distance distribution varies according to particular regional travel patterns. Given this variability, we analyzed the NRRS data in a network setting. We represented visitor home and campground locations as two sets of linked nodes with the strength of each link defined by the number of campers traveling along it. We applied a probabilistic pathway model to the network to identify major vectors of forest insect spread via recreational firewood movement. We estimated the key probability of an individual camper transporting a viable forest insect based on firewood inspections and usage surveys conducted at various state and national parks. Repeated model simulations yielded probabilistic estimates of the most likely pathways and destinations for a forest insect introduced at any origin node. Furthermore, the results provided probabilistic estimates of the most likely origins for any destination node found to be invaded. Such outputs may substantially improve early detection efforts.

The content of this paper reflects the views of the authors(s), who are responsible for the facts and accuracy of the information presented herein.

DIVERSE TRAPS FOR ASIAN LONGHORNED BEETLES

David R. Lance[1], Joseph A. Francese[1], Michael L. Rietz[2],
Damon J. Crook[1], and Victor C. Mastro[1]

[1]USDA APHIS, PPQ, CPHST, Buzzards Bay, MA 02635
[2]USDA APHIS, PPQ, CPHST, Brighton, MI 48116

ABSTRACT

Five types of traps were tested in a newly discovered population of Asian longhorned beetle (ALB), *Anoplophora glabripennis* (Motschulsky), in southeastern Ohio. Traditional woodborer traps (black Intercept panel and 12-funnel bark beetle traps) were compared to traps of several novel designs, including: (1) a modified plum curculio trap, which channel insects crawling up a tree trunk into a capture jar; (2) a "sleeve" trap, which is constructed primarily of screening and also designed to capture insects that are crawling up a trunk, and (3) a 12-funnel trap that is green but otherwise identical to the standard funnel trap. One hundred traps were deployed in 10 blocks, and each block had two of each type of trap, one unbaited and one baited with a standard lure that contained both pheromonal and host-related volatiles.

In total, 162 ALB were caught in 31 traps while 69 of the traps caught no ALB. The distribution was highly skewed with most of the beetles (145) being caught in three blocks, whereas none of the traps in three of the other blocks caught any beetles. The two traditional trap designs appeared to generally outperform traps of alternate design or color, with panel traps averaging 3.1 and black funnel traps averaging 2.5 beetles per trap vs. 0.35 beetles per trap for the green funnel and plum curculio traps. The sleeve traps averaged >2 beetles per trap, but 37 of the 41 beetles they caught were in just 2 of the 20 traps, both in the same block. Overall, the high variability in catch resulted in minimal statistical significance among trap types.

In this test, no apparent effect of the lure was discernible with baited traps capturing a total of 78 beetles, whereas those without lures caught 84 beetles. Although overall catch was low relative to the local ALB population, trapping may still prove useful as a supplement to other methods of surveying for Asian longhorned beetle. Additional tests will be conducted in Ohio, Massachusetts, and China during 2012.

SUCCESSFUL CONTROL OF AN
EMERALD ASH BORER INFESTATION IN WEST VIRGINIA

Phillip A. Lewis[1] and Richard M. Turcotte[2]

[1]USDA APHIS, PPQ, CPHST, Buzzards Bay, MA 02542
[2]U.S. Forest Service, Forest Health Protection, Morgantown, WV 26505

ABSTRACT

Project Background. Emerald ash borer (EAB), *Agrilus planipennis* Fairmaire, was discovered in late 2007 at a recreational area near Oak Hill in Fayette Co., West Virginia. A survey conducted within a ½-mile radius of the original trap tree identified over 300 ash trees (*Fraxinus* spp.), the majority of which showed no signs of EAB infestation. An integrated control and monitoring study was initiated in 2008 due to the following favorable factors: limited ash resource over a large area; isolated and relatively light EAB population; infested ash trees were within a confined area. Ash trees were either cut down and disposed of (149 trees, mostly ≤3" diameter at breast height [d.b.h.]) or treated once by trunk injection in 2008 with emamectin benzoate (Tree-äge®, Arborjet) at varying dosages depending on tree diameter.

Baseline monitoring. Foliar samples from 31 of the treated trees (~20 percent) were collected and analyzed for pesticide residue from 2008 to 2010. Emamectin residue from the 2008 samples was present in significant quantities in all foliage samples, increasing by dosage applied but not differing between sample periods. The average amount of residue found in the foliage ranged between 5 and 8 ppm. Average residue in 2009 was 4-5 percent of the previous year, dropping further to between 2 and 3 percent of the 2008 values by 2010 (Fig. 1).

Twice during each summer over the last four growing seasons, sample trees were assessed for D-shaped exit holes, woodpecker feeding, and general tree health by rating the tree canopy crown. In 2008, about 30 percent of the trees showed evidence of canopy dieback from the August observations. There were very few woodpecker attacks on these trees, and only 6 of the 31 trees had 2-7 putative EAB exit holes, evidence of a light infestation. Additional tree observations during June and August of 2009 evidenced that the trees remain healthy with stable canopy ratings, a 33 to 55 percent decline in observed EAB exit holes and 90 to 100 percent decrease in the number of woodpecker attacks. The trends continued through the current year assessment, with no woodpecker attacks and no visible exit holes for 2011 (Fig. 2).

Assessments. Twelve of the study trees were felled and examined in the fall of 2011 for a more complete assessment of treatment impact and EAB infestation levels. Four trees from each of the three application rates were selected, felled, and debarked to characterize the EAB population within the treated trees. Four control trees from North of Ace that had obvious signs of EAB infestation were used as positive controls by which to compare.

The entire trunk was visually checked for exit holes and was then debarked up to 10 m, with alternate meter sections debarked beyond that. Visual checks were made on all branches >2" in diameter for bark cracking and exit holes. For the control trees, the infestation was so heavy that only a visual check of the trunk was performed for EAB exits and woodpecker attacks, along with a visual check on branches >2" in diameter. For the treated trees, 129 m^2 of log area was processed. No exit holes were found, and only 7 woodpecker attacks (<0.1/m^2) were identified. From all of the bark scraping, only 2 galleries (one a year old) were noted on one of the trees, and no live EAB larvae were found. In contrast, control trees had 36 m^2 of log area processed, and 392 EAB exit holes (11/m^2) and 2,232 woodpecker attacks (62/m^2) were identified.

The results of this study demonstrate that there are situations where EAB populations can be managed. An integrated approach of phloem reduction (removal of small diameter trees and felling and surface treatments of infested trees) and insecticide treatment can provide multi-year protection of the ash resource from EAB attack. Although the ultimate outcome of EAB on ash may not change, integrated approaches using currently available tools can provide land managers with options to remove and retain trees as desired. Thinning, timber stand improvement, and crop tree techniques in concert with an integrated management approach can be used to control the mortality trajectory of EAB and manage canopy disturbance and treefall.

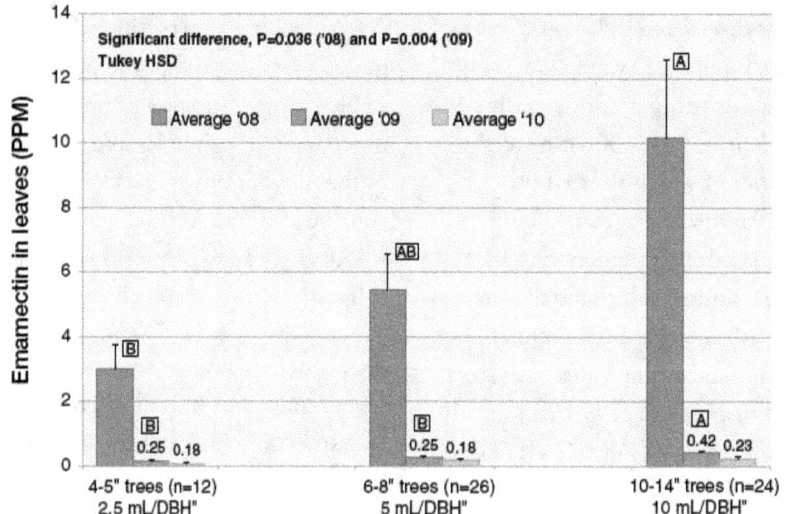

Figure 1.—Pesticide residue data from foliage of treated trees.

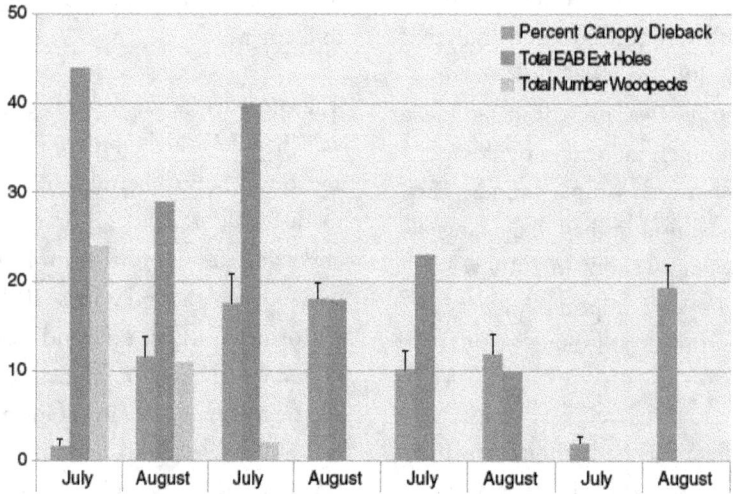

Figure 2.—Tree health and infestation level ratings post application.

The content of this paper reflects the views of the authors(s), who are responsible for the facts and accuracy of the information presented herein.

ASIAN LONGHORNED BEETLE (ALB), *ANOPLOPHORA GLABRIPENNIS*, ERADICATION PROGRAM

Christine Markham[1] and Brendon Reardon[2]

[1]USDA APHIS, Raleigh, NC 27606
[2]USDA APHIS, Riverdale, MD 20737

ABSTRACT

Asian longhorned beetle (ALB), *Anoplophora glabripennis*, detections in the United States include Brooklyn, NY (August 1996), Chicago, IL (July 1998), Jersey City, NJ (October 2002), Worcester, MA (August 2008), and Bethel, OH (June 2011). The eradication program declared eradication of infestations in Chicago and Jersey City in 2008 and in Islip, NY in 2011. There are currently 336 mi^2 regulated for ALB in the United States including 135 mi^2 in New York, 25 mi^2 in New Jersey, 120 mi^2 in Massachusetts, and 56 mi^2 in Ohio. In New York, survey inspections continue. The last detection was on April 26, 2010, in Brooklyn, and confirmation surveys for declaring eradication of New York County began in August 2011. A total of 6,275 infested trees have been detected, 18,467 infested and high-risk host trees have been removed, and 30,131 trees were treated in 2011. In New Jersey, survey inspections continue. The last detection was on August 1, 2006 in Linden, and confirmation surveys for declaring eradication of Middlesex and Union counties began in September 2011. To date, 729 infested trees have been detected, and 21,981 infested and high-risk host trees have been removed. Treatment applications were finished in 2009. In Massachusetts, survey inspections continue, and over 1.8 million host trees have been surveyed. More than 20,430 infested trees have been detected, and over 30,480 infested and high-risk host trees have been removed. A total of 137,177 trees were treated in 2011. In Ohio, survey inspections continue, and more than 70,000 host trees have been surveyed, over 4,700 infested trees have been detected, and over 781 trees have been removed. The goal of the ALB program is to eradicate the pest in the United States to protect the hardwood forests of North America. To achieve this goal, the ALB program has developed and implemented eradication protocols, using an area-wide, science-based strategy, including: exclusion, visual survey of host trees, tree removal, chemical treatment, regulatory activities to prevent the pest's spread, replanting to mitigate effects of trees lost to ALB, outreach efforts, quality assurance to ensure survey, removals, and treatments are done correctly so that these actions are effective, and methods development to improve program effectiveness and delivery.

EFFECT OF DEBARKING AND HEATING ON SURVIVAL OF THE THOUSAND CANKERS DISEASE VECTOR AND PATHOGEN IN BLACK WALNUT LOGS

Albert E. Mayfield III[1], Adam Taylor[2], Stephen Fraedrich[1], Paul Merten[3], and Darren Bailey[4]

[1] U.S. Forest Service, Southern Research Station, Ashville, NC 28804
[2] University of Tennessee, Center for Renewable Carbon, Knoxville, TN 37996
[3] U.S. Forest Service, Forest Health Protection, Ashville, NC 28804
[4] Tennessee Division of Forestry, Knoxville, TN 37901

ABSTRACT

Thousand cankers disease (TCD) is a fatal disease of black walnut (*Juglans nigra* L.), caused by attacks of the walnut twig beetle (*Pityophtorus juglandis*) and associated infection with a canker-causing fungus (*Geosmithia morbida*) on branches and stems. Phytosanitary tools allowing movement of walnut logs without spreading the TCD vector or pathogen are needed in the commercial walnut industry. This study evaluated heat and debarking for efficacy in eliminating the walnut twig beetle and *G. morbida* from small black walnut logs. A total of 150 black walnut logs (3-7 inches diameter, 12 inches long) were cut from TCD-symptomatic trees, and 30 logs were exposed to one of the following five treatments in both June and August, 2011: 1) kiln heated at 60 °C for 30 minutes, 2) kiln heated at 65 °C for 30 minutes, 3) kiln heated at 70 °C for 30 minutes, 4) debarked by hand with a chisel, and 5) control. Actual heat treatment times ranged from 30-40 minutes. In each treatment group, 10 logs were sampled for pathogen pre- and posttreatment, and 20 logs were placed in rearing containers and monitored for insect emergence. In the June 2011 trial, *G. morbida* was recovered posttreatment only from control and debarked logs, but was present in 40-100 percent of pretreatment logs in all treatments. *Geosmithia morbida* was not isolated from posttreatment logs of any heat treatment in either trial. No live beetles of any species emerged from heat-treated logs, whereas live beetles emerged from 75-90 percent of control logs. Walnut twig beetle did not emerge from control logs in the June trial but emerged from 20 percent of control logs in the August trial. Only ambrosia beetles (sapwood borers) emerged from debarked logs. Time required to heat logs to the target temperature, at both the outer sapwood and the log core, increased with log diameter. Heating the outer sapwood to 60 °C, 65 °C, or 70 °C for 40 minutes is sufficient to kill *G. morbida* in small black walnut logs, whereas debarking does not ensure elimination of the pathogen. The three heat treatments eliminated all live beetles from all logs, but because walnut twig beetles emerged from a low percentage of control logs, follow-up work is planned to more conclusively evaluate the effect of heat treatments on the walnut twig beetle and the minimum effective temperatures for eliminating both disease agents.

EFFECT OF HIGH TEMPERATURES
ON AESTIVATING HEMLOCK WOOLLY ADELGID

Angela M. Mech[1], Robert O. Teskey[1], J. Rusty Rhea[2], and Kamal J.K. Gandhi[1]

[1]University of Georgia, Warnell School of Forestry and Natural Resources, Athens, GA 30602
[2]U.S. Forest Service, Forest Health Protection, Asheville, NC 28802

ABSTRACT

The hemlock woolly adelgid (HWA), *Adelges tsugae* Annand (Hemiptera: Adelgidae), is an exotic sap-sucking insect that is causing widespread mortality of eastern (*Tsuga canadensis* [L.] Carr.) and Carolina (*Tsuga caroliniana* Engelm.) hemlocks in North America. The life cycle of HWA includes two parthenogenetic generations on hemlock, sisten and progredien, with summer dormancy (aestivation) lasting up to 5 months. We observed unexpected trends at low elevation sites (<500 m) in Georgia where hemlocks were in low decline following 6-7 years of HWA infestation instead of anticipated mortality 3-5 years post infestation. A controlled experiment was designed to test if high temperatures and lengths of heat waves experienced during summer months in Georgia may affect aestivating HWA sisten survivorship. During the summer of 2011, approximately 240 twigs with aestivating HWA sistens were collected from eastern hemlock trees in northern Georgia. Live sistens were selected (n=4,279), and twigs were then randomly placed in one of the temperature (20, 25, 30, 35, or 40 °C) by length of time in chamber (2, 4, 6, or 8 days) treatment combinations. Overall, a total of 1,972 sistens did not survive the temperature treatments, with the majority of the mortality occurring at 35 °C (93.8 percent) and 40 °C (97.2 percent). Logistic regression showed a significant ($p < 0.001$) positive correlation between increasing temperature and percent HWA mortality. At 20 and 25 °C, the duration in the growth chamber did not have a significant effect on HWA mortality. However, there was a significant correlation between the duration held at 30 °C and percent HWA mortality (20 percent mortality at 2 days increasing to 48 percent mortality at 8 days). Aestivating HWA sistens experienced 100 percent mortality by 4 days at both 35 and 40 °C. Results from this experiment will contribute to future climatic models that will more accurately predict ecological impacts of exotic insects, and further aid in the management of HWA by predicting locations where biological control may have more time to become effective.

MONITORING OF ASIAN LONGHORNED BEETLES IN WORCESTER, MASSACHUSETTS USING PHEROMONE AND KAIROMONE BLENDS

Peter S. Meng[1], Maya E. Nehme[1], Melody A. Keena[2], R. Talbot Trotter[2], Clint D. McFarland[3], Alan J. Sawyer[4], and Kelli Hoover[1]

[1]Pennsylvania State University, Department of Entomology and Center for Chemical Ecology, University Park, PA 16802-1009
[2]U.S. Forest Service, Northern Research Station, Hamden, CT 06514-1703
[3]USDA APHIS, Cooperative ALB Eradication Program, Worcester, MA 01606-2753
[4]USDA APHIS, PPQ, CPHST, Buzzards Bay, MA 02542-1308

ABSTRACT

Development of an effective trapping system to detect *Anoplophora glabripennis*, the Asian longhorned beetle (ALB), has been a goal of the U.S. Department of Agriculture eradication program since beetles were discovered in New York City in 1996. Without eradication, ALB is estimated to kill 30 percent of all urban trees, resulting in $669 billion in losses. To detect infestations, ground surveyors and climbers search for oviposition pits and exit holes. However, ground surveys are 30 percent effective at best, and climbing is labor intensive and expensive. Trapping is a cost effective, efficient means of guiding surveyors and climbers towards infestations over large geographic areas. A previously identified two component male produced pheromone (MP) consisting of an aldehyde and alcohol 4-(n-heptyloxy)butanal and 4-(n-heptyloxy)butan-1-ol has been utilized in previous trapping studies. The MP is almost entirely attractive to females.

Addition of maple plant volatile mixes (±)-linalool, (Z)-3-hexen-1-ol, linalool oxide, *β*-caryophyllene, and *trans*-pinocarveol to MP-baited traps significantly increased catches of virgin females in China and Worcester, MA during previous field seasons. The goal of this project was to test low and high release rates of MP and various combinations of maple plant volatiles in a large-scale deployment of traps across previously infested surveyed and unsurveyed areas throughout the Greater Worcester, MA (Worcester, Boylston, West Boylston, Holden, Shrewsbury, Auburn) quarantine area to detect ALB. A total of 23 beetles were caught during the summer of 2011, including 21 females and 2 males. High pheromone release rates increased beetle catches in nonhost trees. Removal of *trans*-pinocarveol and linalool oxide from the lures and altering ratios of the other three kairomones increased trap catches.

PARASITIC *DELADENUS* NEMATODES IN EASTERN NORTH AMERICAN *SIREX* SPECIES

E. Erin Morris[1], Ryan M. Kepler[1], Stefan J. Long[1], David W. Williams[2], and Ann E. Hajek[1]

[1]Cornell University, Department of Entomology, Ithaca, NY 14853-2601
[2]USDA APHIS, PPQ, Buzzards Bay, MA 02542

ABSTRACT

Sirex noctilio is an invasive pest of pine (*Pinus* spp.) trees that was first collected in New York State in 2004 and currently threatens 200 million hectares of U.S. and Canadian pines. Also an invasive pest in the Southern Hemisphere, in many cases *S. noctilio* has been successfully controlled in a biological control program using the parasitic nematode *Deladenus siricidicola* Kamona strain (initially Sopron strain). The North American invasion is the first introduction of *S. noctilio* to a location where *Sirex* and conifer hosts are native, which increases the complexity of developing a control program. The native North American *Sirex* species carry their own nematodes which are difficult to distinguish morphologically from the strain of *D. siricidicola* that would be used for biological control.

Additionally, *S. noctilio* in North America has been found to carry a nonsterilizing strain of *D. siricidicola* which is presumed to have arrived with the invasion. In order to characterize the nematode diversity in eastern North American *Sirex* woodwasps, as well as to develop methods to distinguish the different species and strains of nematodes, we extracted nematode DNA from the following parasitized *Sirex* hosts: *S. noctilio*, *S. cyaneus*, *S. nitidus*, and *S. nigricornis*. Two nuclear (28S and ITS) and one mitochondrial (CO1) gene were amplified and sequenced. Phylogenetic reconstructions were performed using maximum likelihood (ML) in the program RAxML. Four major groups of *Deladenus*, possibly representing four different species were found, each principally associated with a different *Sirex* species.

EMERALD ASH BORER IN TENNESSEE: A SOUTHERN PERSPECTIVE

Steve D. Powell[1], Kenneth J. Copley[2], and Jerome F. Grant[3]

[1]Tennessee Department of Agriculture, Division of Regulatory Services, Nashville, TN 37204
[2]USDA APHIS, PPQ, Murfreesboro, TN 37130
[3]The University of Tennessee, Department of Entomology and Plant Pathology,
Knoxville, TN 37996-4560

ABSTRACT

Emerald ash borer (EAB), *Agrilus planipennis*, an invasive wood-boring beetle native to Asia, threatens the ash (*Fraxinus* spp.) resources in North America, especially in the United States. This exotic pest was first discovered near Detroit, MI in 2002 and has since spread to 15 states where millions of trees have died. The potential distribution of EAB in the United States includes all areas where ash species grow. In 2010, infestations of this devastating pest were found in Tennessee, the southernmost documentation of this invasive insect species. Efforts were initiated to enhance our knowledge of this beetle in Tennessee so we can make informed management and regulatory decisions. This paper details efforts to assess the incidence and distribution of EAB in Tennessee.

Emerald ash borer was positively identified on ash trees at a truck stop in Knox County, Tennessee, in 2010. USDA APHIS Plant Protection and Quarantine (PPQ) and Tennessee Department of Agriculture personnel immediately initiated a 3-week visual survey and documented EAB in two counties (Knox and Loudon Co). To further assess distribution in Tennessee, trapping programs were conducted in 2011, emphasizing the eastern part of the state where the insect was first found. During 2011, a total of 3,558 EAB traps were placed in 75 counties throughout Tennessee.

Although extensive trapping was conducted in 2011, especially in eastern Tennessee, only four additional county infestations were documented (Blount, Claiborne, Grainger, and Sevier). Thus, six counties (two counties in 2010; four counties in 2011) were quarantined and the movement of wood products was restricted. While most traps collected only 1 or 2 adults, the traps near the original 2010 site caught as many as 37 adults in a single trap.

Declining and dying trees at the original site in Knox County suggest that EAB has been present in Tennessee for at least 5 years. A dendrochronological analysis of the EAB detection in one county (Claiborne) was conducted by James Buck (Program Analyst, USDA APHIS). This analysis indicated that this stand of ash was infested by at least 2007 (4-year-old infestation site). The documentation of EAB (n=1) in Sevier County is significant because this county includes part of the Great Smoky Mountains National Park. More extensive trapping will be conducted in this county in 2012 to clearly define the distribution of EAB in this area.

The presence of EAB in Tennessee represents the most southern distribution of this invasive pest in the United States. Research is underway to further assess the incidence, distribution, and impact of EAB in Tennessee, as well as assess the role of biological control agents in reducing its populations. Quarantine efforts are underway to limit the spread of this pest, and additional trapping will be conducted in 2012 to further confirm its distribution in the state.

INUNDATIVE RELEASE OF *APHTHONA* SPP. FLEA BEETLES (COLEOPTERA: CHRYSOMELIDAE) AS A BIOLOGICAL "HERBICIDE" ON LEAFY SPURGE (*EUPHORBIA ESULA* L.) IN RIPARIAN AREAS

Roger A. Progar[1], G.P. Markin[2], Joseph Milan[3], Thomas Barbouletos[4], and Matthew J. Rinella[5]

[1] U.S. Forest Service, Pacific Northwest Research Station, La Grande, OR 97850
[2] U.S. Forest Service, Rocky Mountain Research Station, Bozeman, MT 59717 (retired)
[3] Bureau of Land Management, Boise District, Boise, ID 83709
[4] U.S. Forest Service, Forest Health Protection, Kalispell, MT 59901
[5] USDA ARS, Livestock and Range Research Laboratory, Miles City, MT 59301

ABSTRACT

Inundative releases of beneficial insects are frequently used to suppress pest insects, but they are not commonly attempted as a method of weed biological control because of the difficulty in obtaining the required large numbers of insects. The successful establishment of a flea beetle complex (87 percent *Aphthona lacertosa* and 13 percent *A. nigriscutus*) for the control of leafy spurge (*Euphorbia esula* L.) provided an easily collectable source of these natural enemies that enabled us to attempt inundative release as a possible leafy spurge control method in a sensitive riparian ecological zone where chemical control is restricted. Our target weed populations were small, isolated patches of leafy spurge along three streams in southwestern, central, and northeastern Idaho.

This study assessed leafy spurge and associated vegetation responses to inundative releases of 10 and 50 beetles per spurge flowering stem over 2 consecutive years. Releasing 10 beetles per flowering stem had inconclusive effects on spurge biomass, crown, stem, and seedling density. Alternatively, releasing 50 beetles per flowering stem resulted in a 60-80 percent reduction of biomass, crown, and stem density in at all three study sites and about a 60 percent reduction of seedling density at one site, compared to untreated plots. In contrast to leafy spurge, associated vegetation did not conclusively respond to beetle release, indicating that it may take more than 2 years for desired riparian vegetation to respond to reductions in leafy spurge competition.

ADVANCEMENTS IN ERADICATION IN THE ASIAN LONGHORNED BEETLE (ALB) PROGRAM THROUGH 2011

Brendon Reardon[1] and Christine Markham[2]

[1]USDA APHIS, Riverdale, MD 20737
[2]USDA APHIS, Raleigh, NC 27606

ABSTRACT

Asian longhorned beetle (ALB), *Anoplophora glabripennis*, detections in the United States include Brooklyn, NY (August 1996), Chicago, IL (July 1998), Jersey City, NJ (October 2002), Worcester, MA (August 2008), and Bethel, OH (June 2011). ALB has the potential to be one of the most destructive and costly invasive species to enter the United States. Industries at risk include timber export, saw logs, fuel wood, nursery stock, lumber and veneer, pulp and paper, home construction, plywood, firewood, fine furniture and cabinet making, maple syrup, and fall foliage tourism. ALB also has the potential to cause significant ecological and environmental impacts. The goal of the ALB program is to eradicate this pestiferous beetle in the United States to protect forest products industries, U.S. hardwood forests and park lands, and the quality of the urban environment. To achieve this goal, the ALB program has developed and implemented area-wide, science-based eradication protocols. The eradication strategy is based on a combination of tactics, including: 1) exclusion; 2) visual survey of host trees; 3) infested and high-risk host tree removal; 4) chemical treatment; 5) regulatory activities to thwart the artificial spread of ALB; 6) replanting to mitigate the effects of trees lost to ALB; 7) outreach and education activities; 8) quality assurance to ensure survey, removals, and treatments are conducted correctly to maintain effectiveness; and 9) methods development to improve program efficacy and delivery. In 2008, the ALB program declared eradication of infestations in Chicago, IL and Jersey City, NJ and declared eradication in Islip, NY in 2011. As of December 31, 2011, a total of 336 square miles are regulated for ALB in the United States. New York has 135 square miles under quarantine. The ALB program continues to conduct survey activities in Manhattan, parts of Brooklyn and Queens, and an area along the Nassau-Suffolk County line on Long Island. In August 2011, a final survey was initiated and is ongoing to confirm eradication of ALB in Manhattan. A total of 6,275 infested trees have been detected, and 18,467 infested and high-risk host trees have been removed in New York overall. In 2011, approximately 30,131 host trees in Brooklyn, Western Queens, and Staten Island received prophylactic chemical treatment. New Jersey has 25 square miles under quarantine. Survey of host trees continues with the last detection of an infested tree being made in August 2006. Overall, approximately 729 infested trees have been detected, and 21,981 infested and high-risk host trees have been removed in New Jersey. Preventative chemical applications were finished in 2009. In September 2011, a final survey was initiated and is ongoing to confirm eradication of ALB in New Jersey. Massachusetts has 120 square miles under quarantine. Surveys continue to delimit the infestation, and over 1.8 million host trees have been evaluated. Over 20,500 infested trees have been detected, and over 30,500 infested and high-risk host trees have been removed. In 2011, a total of 137,177 host trees received treatment in Massachusetts. Ohio has 56 square miles under quarantine. Delimitation surveys continue to delineate the infestation. Over 76,000 host trees have been surveyed, and more than 5,100 infested trees have been detected. Over 1,100 infested trees have been removed.

EFFECTS OF SOIL CALCIUM ON PLANT INVASIONS AND BREEDING FOREST BIRDS: A FRAME STUDY-FOREST FRAGMENTS IN MANAGED ECOSYSTEMS

Christine Rega[1], W. Gregory Shriver[1], and Vincent D'Amico[2]

[1]University of Delaware, Department of Entomology and Wildlife Ecology, Newark, DE 19716
[2]U.S. Forest Service, Northern Research Station Newark, DE 19716

ABSTRACT

The effects of decreased soil calcium availability have recently been called to attention for driving migrant bird declines. Multiple studies have shown a strong relationship between avian reproductive success and the availability of calcium; however few studies have demonstrated trends in multiple avian species habitat preference in relation to natural soil calcium characteristics. In this study, we asked how the availability of soil calcium affects snail abundance, understory vegetation, and breeding forest bird territory density in urban forest fragments. In 2010 and 2011, we sampled 21 forest fragment sites in Newark, DE, to estimate soil calcium, vegetation composition, snail abundance, and avian territory density. Within these plots, we randomly sampled for soil composition; snail abundance and weight; and vegetation cover, composition, and nativity. We mapped breeding bird territories based on 10 visits to each site (May-July). The calcium:aluminum ratio (Ca:Al) was used as an ecological threshold (Ca:Al $\geq$ 1) to assess the acidity of forest systems. Solubility of aluminum (A^{3+}) increases in acidic soils, consequently reducing the availability of calcium by disrupting calcium membrane transport. We used analysis of variance (ANOVA) to compare snail abundance and vegetation cover between calcium-poor (Ca:Al < 1) and calcium-rich (Ca:Al $\geq$ 1) sites.

In addition, we utilized the unmarked package in R to fit hierarchical models to the bird count data to estimate abundance while accounting for observational and site covariates. We also used linear regressions to determine if the shrub nativity predicted the territory densities of the observed bird species at the site level. We found that snail abundance was 2.4 times greater in sites with Ca:Al $\geq$ 1 ($F_{1,19}$ = 14.03; $P < 0.001$). We also found that nonnative plant cover was 2.6 times greater in sites with Ca:Al $\geq$ 1 ($F_{1,19}$ = 36.58; $P < 0.001$). Soil calcium did not serve as the top model to determine any species abundance, nor did the percentage of nonnative stems. However, Northern cardinals (*Cardinalis cardinalis*; r^2 = 0.61, β = 0.078, $P < 0.001$), Carolina wrens (*Thryothorus ludovicianus*; r^2 = 0.42, β = 0.156, $P = 0.001$), and Carolina chickadees (*Poecile carolinensis*; r^2 = 0.25, β = 0.098, $P = 0.021$) had a positive relationship with the mean percentage of nonnative stems within the site, while brown-headed cowbirds (*Molothrus ater*; r^2 = 0.24, β = -0.668, $P = 0.023$) and ovenbirds (*Seiurus aurocapillus*; r^2 = 0.19, β = -0.07, $P = 0.05$) were negatively related. With these results, we have evidence that few species can be limited by natural changes in soil calcium availability, as well as other landscape variables.

EUROPEAN EARTHWORM INVASION PATTERNS WITHIN NATIONAL WILDLIFE REFUGES OF THE UPPER GREAT LAKES

Lindsey M. Shartell[1], R. Gregory Corace III[2], and Andrew J. Storer[1]

[1]Michigan Technological University, School of Forest Resources and Environmental Science, Houghton, MI 49931
[2]U.S. Fish and Wildlife Service, Seney National Wildlife Refuge, Seney, MI 49883

ABSTRACT

The invasion of exotic earthworms into forested ecosystems in the Great Lakes region threatens to cause detrimental changes to the forest understory and soils. These changes are suspected to have cascading negative impacts within these ecosystems. How higher-level landscape scale patterns, in combination with forest and soil characteristics, influence earthworm abundance and community composition across the landscape is not fully understood. This research examines patterns of earthworm abundance and community composition to deduce potential drivers and constraints of earthworm invasion and identify specific environmental correlates. It was hypothesized that stand level environmental variables associated with earthworm habitat suitability and dispersal opportunity would be correlated with earthworm biomass and community composition and that landscape level patterns dominated by the presence of anthropogenic cover types would increase earthworm biomass and diversity. Four stand level variables were found to be associated with increased earthworm biomass: high soil pH, high basal area of earthworm preferred species, high percent anthropogenic cover, and low conifer dominance. In addition, canonical correspondence analysis indicated that these variables along with proximity to agriculture influence earthworm community composition. At the landscape level, increasing earthworm abundance was correlated with increasing mean patch area of anthropogenic cover. Grouping earthworms into functional groups, however, revealed differences in the influence of anthropogenic landscape patterns, with epi-endogeic species found to be the only group significantly associated with anthropogenic land cover. Contradictory to our hypothesis, earthworm community diversity was greatest in areas with a variety of natural land cover components rather than those areas homogenized by anthropogenic lands. These results improve our understanding of the invasion patterns, habitat preferences, and potential impacts of exotic earthworms in Great Lakes forests. This knowledge, in turn, may drive forest management decisions to mitigate negative impacts and sustain ecosystem health.

FIVE *FRAXINUS* SPECIES AND ONE *AGRILUS* BEETLE: ADULT EMERALD ASH BORER SURVIVAL, HOST PREFERENCE, AND LARVAL DENSITY

Sara R. Tanis[1] and Deborah G. McCullough[1,2]

[1] Michigan State University, Department of Forestry, East Lansing, MI 48824
[2] Michigan State University, Department of Entomology, East Lansing, MI 48824

ABSTRACT

Emerald ash borer (EAB), *Agrilus planipennis* Fairmaire (Coleoptera: Buprestidae), is an invasive exotic insect pest that has killed tens of millions of ash (*Fraxinus* spp.) trees in North America. North American ash trees lack a coevolutionary history with EAB, which likely accounts for high ash mortality in North America. There are at least 16 native *Fraxinus* species, and all are likely susceptible to EAB infestation. Asian ash trees, however, share a coevolutionary history with EAB and, in its native range, EAB only colonizes dying or severely stressed trees. In North America, EAB attacks healthy and stressed *Fraxinus* trees, regardless of genetic origin.

Female EAB feed for approximately 1 week before mating and feed 2 more weeks before oviposition begins. They continue to feed and likely oviposit on trees where they feed. Larvae must develop within trees chosen by their mothers, regardless of host suitability. Therefore, adult feeding preference is important because it influences host selection for oviposition and possibly larval survival.

The purpose of our study was to assess:

- adult *A. planipennis* host feeding preference, and

- adult survival and larval density across five evolutionarily diverse *Fraxinus* species from North America (*F. quadrangulata*, *F. americana*, *F. pennsylvanica*, and *F. nigra*) and Asia (*F. mandshurica*).

In 2006, a total of 225 *Fraxinus* trees were planted in a randomized complete block design at the Tree Research Center (TRC), Michigan State University, in Okemos, MI. The common garden consisted of 45 trees of each of the five *Fraxinus* species. Each spring until 2010, trees were wrapped with screen wire and tree wrap to prevent colonization by wild EAB.

Feeding Bioassays: In June 2010, leaves were collected from trees and brought back to the laboratory. A section was removed from each leaf, weighed, and scanned. Immediately after scanning, leaf stems were placed into a water pic, and leaf sections were positioned inside a petri dish. Four newly emerged, unfed beetles (2 males + 2 females) were added to each petri dish. Beetles fed on foliage for 4 days, after which foliage was removed, weighed, and rescanned. Beetle mortality was recorded daily. Results indicated that, on average, EAB adults consumed less foliage from black and blue ash trees than Manchurian ash and white ash trees. Consumption of green ash tree foliage was intermediate.

Mortality Bioassays: Upon completion of 4-day feeding bioassays, surviving beetles were transferred to new petri dishes and provided with fresh foliage every other day for 10 additional days. Mortality was recorded during each foliage change. Less than 40 percent of adult EAB that fed on blue ash foliage would have lived long enough to mate and lay eggs. In contrast, beetles that fed on Manchurian ash foliage had the highest rates of survival (89 percent). Beetles caged on green, white, or black ash foliage had intermediate survival rates.

Larval Density: In October 2010, after one season of exposure to wild EAB populations, trees were destructively harvested and tree boles were carefully peeled using a draw knife. Outer layers of bark and phloem were removed to expose galleries. Number of larvae, woodpeckers, exit holes, and larval instar were recorded. Green ash trees were heavily attacked, averaging more than 250 galleries per m^2. Manchurian ash, a "resistant" Asian species, had roughly 30 galleries per m^2, but that was three-fold higher than blue ash trees, which averaged less than 11 galleries per m^2.

Larval density on black ash and white ash trees were intermediate but averaged over 100 larvae per m^2, which is high enough to cause tree mortality.

Our results indicated that while Manchurian ash is considered a resistant species in its native range, EAB adults readily consumed Manchurian ash foliage and adult survival was high. However, larval gallery density was low, indicating that resistance mechanisms are likely present in phloem. Blue ash foliage was readily consumed by adult EAB, but beetle survival was relatively poor, and these trees had the lowest larval densities. Despite a lack of coevolution with EAB, North American blue ash was the least vulnerable of the five *Fraxinus* species evaluated.

COMPARING FUNGAL BAND FORMULATIONS
FOR ASIAN LONGHORNED BEETLE BIOLOGICAL CONTROL

Todd A. Ugine[1], Nina Jenkins[2], and Ann E. Hajek[1]

[1]Cornell University, Department of Entomology, Ithaca, NY 14853
[2]Pennsylvania State University, Department of Entomology, University Park PA 16802

ABSTRACT

Fungal bands (fabric supporting cultures of entomopathogenic fungi) are used to manage a variety of cerambycid pests in Asia and have been shown to reduce the number of oviposition pits and exit wounds created by Asian longhorned beetles (ALB), Anoplophora glabripennis, on banded trees. The production of agar-based fungal bands is labor intensive. By growing conidia on grains such as barley and formulating them in oil, large numbers of bands can be produced without the fussiness of physically growing and drying the fungal culture on the band material. Experiments were conducted to determine the feasibility of using oil-formulated fungal bands versus traditional agar-based bands. We investigated conidial retention and survival on three types of bands hung in the field: our traditional polyester fiber agar-based bands, traditional polyester bands formulated with oil, and burlap bands formulated in oil. Fungal bands were produced at the Pennsylvania State University by growing fungal cultures within the bands (traditional material-agar) and by dipping band material in an oil-conidia suspension (traditional material-oil and burlap-oil). Bands hung on trees in Ithaca, NY and in State College, PA during the summer of 2010 were sampled every 7–14 days for a total of 8–9 weeks. The number and viability of conidia per cm^2 of fungal band was determined for five replicate bands of each band type. Band formulation did not affect the number or viability of conidia over the test period. We also assessed the effect of band formulation on conidial acquisition by adult beetles in cages containing fungal bands. A beetle was introduced into the bottom of each cage, collected after 24 h and washed with dichloromethane. The number of conidia per beetle was determined. Significantly more conidia were acquired by ALB from agar bands, despite their having the fewest conidia/cm^2 of band. Rates of adult beetle mortality were assessed after adults were made to walk over 15 cm of the three types of fungal bands. A subset of beetles was washed with dichloromethane immediately after crossing the band for estimates of conidial acquisition, and the remainder of the beetles were held at 25 °C for 8 weeks, and mortality was monitored daily. Traditional material-agar bands both delivered the most conidia to beetles and killed beetles significantly faster compared to the other two band formulations.

FUNGAL BAND ARCHITECTURE AND FORMULATION FOR ASIAN LONGHORNED BEETLE BIOLOGICAL CONTROL

Todd A. Ugine[1], Nina Jenkins[2], and Ann E. Hajek[1]

[1]Cornell University, Department of Entomology, Ithaca, NY 14853
[2]Pennsylvania State University, Department of Entomology, University Park, PA 16802

ABSTRACT

Fungal bands containing entomopathogenic fungi are used to manage pestiferous cerambycids and have been tested against Asian longhorned beetles (ALB), *Anoplophora glabripennis*. Commercially-produced bands are made from relatively flat material (2-3 mm height). Because beetles need to walk over a fungal band to acquire a lethal dosage of conidia, the development of fungal band formulations that deliver more conidia to beetles is desirable. Fungal bands can be produced by growing an agar-based fungal culture directly in/on the band or by spraying/dipping band material in an oil-conidia suspension. We tested four different oil-formulated materials (terry cloth; cotton bath robe; 3 cm-long cotton spikes, and 3 cm-long polyester spikes, each sprayed with 5 ml of 10^9 conidia/ml in 4:1 Isopar M:Ondina oil) to investigate dose acquisition and rates of mortality by adult ALB. We found that material type did not significantly affect conidial acquisition, although the cotton spikes delivered 2-3 times more conidia. Beetles crossing polyester bands lived the longest, and there were no differences in the survivorship curves of the remaining materials. We examined the behavioral response of adult beetles to the blank oil formulation on polyester batting, terry cloth, 3 cm cotton spikes, and 1.5 cm cotton spikes that were all soaked in 4:1 Isopar M:Ondina oil, wrung out and dried 4 d in a fume hood and compared these with 'dry' unformulated bands. More adult ALB failed to cross oil-formulated versus dry bands. Dry unformulated cotton spikes were difficult to cross due to the lack of rigidity provided by agar-formulation as per the following test. Based on the results from these experiments, we tested the effect of flat (2-3 mm height) versus spiky (3 cm height) agar-based fungal bands on dose acquisition and rates of adult beetle mortality. Adult beetles were placed at the bottom of fungal-banded cardboard tubes and allowed to walk over 5 cm of fungal band. A subset of beetles was washed with dichloromethane immediately after crossing the band for estimates of conidial acquisition (conidia per insect). The remaining beetles were held at 25 °C for 4 weeks, and mortality was monitored daily. Spiky bands delivered nine times more conidia to adult beetles, and the rate of death of beetles walking over spiky bands was significantly faster compared to flat bands (median survival time of ca. 9 versus 17 d).

COMPARISON OF BEECH BARK DISEASE DISTRIBUTION AND IMPACTS IN MICHIGAN FROM 2002 TO 2011

James B. Wieferich[1] and Deborah G. McCullough[1,2]

[1]Michigan State University, Department of Entomology, East Lansing, MI 43324
[2]Michigan State University, Department of Forestry, East Lansing, MI 48824

ABSTRACT

Beech bark disease (BBD) has spread across much of the northern range of American Beech (*Fagus grandifolia* Ehrh.) since its arrival in eastern Canada around 1890. The nonindigenous beech scale, *Cryptoccus fagisuga* Lind., colonizes the outer bark of beech trees, facilitating the entry of the cambium-killing *Neonectria* spp. pathogen. Three stages of BBD have been recognized. The advancing front refers to stands where trees are infested by beech scale, the killing front refers to stands where trees are dying from the *Neonectria* infection, and the aftermath forest refers to stands that have experience the impacts resulting from BBD.

Infestations of beech scale were first identified in one Lower and one Upper Michigan County in 2000. In 2002-2003, impact plots were established in 62 sites in 22 counties. The sites represented stands that were uninfested, lightly infested, and heavily infested with beech scale and stands with low, moderate, or high beech densities. At that time, impacts of BBD were minimal and data collected during impact surveys represent baseline conditions. In 2010-2011, we revisited 60 of the 62 impact plots to quantify current beech scale densities, overstory condition, understory vegetation, and down woody debris. Current conditions were compared to variables recorded in 2002-2003 to assess effects of BBD on stand composition, productivity, and wildlife-related variables.

Since 2002, beech scale densities have increased across all infested locations, and many uninfested sites have been colonized. The advancing front has spread from the original discovery in 2 counties to 24 counties in 2011. Surveys in 2005 showed approximately 2,650 km^2 and 6,200 km^2 were infested with beech scale in Lower and Upper Michigan, respectively. In 2011, the areas encompassing beech scale infestations had grown to approximately 7,900 km^2 and 12,200 km^2 in Lower and Upper Michigan, respectively. Heavy infestations around roads and campgrounds suggest human traffic plays a role in beech scale distribution.

High beech mortality was observed in areas with heavy beech scale infestations, but beech mortality rates in Lower Michigan are substantially lower than in Upper Michigan. Overall, 25.5 percent and 10 percent of overstory beech trees were dead in Upper and Lower Michigan, respectively. In the Upper Michigan stands that were infested in 2003, roughly 40 percent of beech trees were dead in 2011, compared to only 13 percent of trees in previously infested stands in Lower Michigan. Approximately 25 percent of 700 pieces of down woody material pieces in our stands were >20 cm in diameter. Most of the down woody debris was fresh (64 percent), while 11 percent was severely decayed and 25 percent was intermediate.

Beech seedlings were present in 59 of the 62 sites, but maple (*Acer* spp.) and white ash (*Fraxinus Americana* L.) seedlings dominated regeneration, accounting for more than 85 and 75 percent of all seedlings in Upper and Lower Michigan sites, respectively. Beech dominated the sapling stratum, accounting for 63 percent of all saplings, followed by maple (21.5 percent) and ironwood (7.1 percent). Maple and beech were also the most abundant recruits in all stands. Few beech thickets were observed, and all were in Upper Michigan.

HUMAN-ASSISTED SPREAD OF EMERALD ASH BORER VIA A ROAD NETWORK: ASSESSING PEST RISKS WITH A PORTFOLIO VALUATION TECHNIQUE

Denys Yemshanov[1], Frank H. Koch[2], Barry Lyons[1], Mark Ducey[3], and Klaus Koehler[4]

Canadian Forest Service, Great Lakes Forestry Centre, Sault Ste. Marie, ON, P6A2E5
[2]U.S. Forest Service, Southern Research Station, Research Triangle Park, NC 27709
[3]University of New Hampshire, Natural Resources and the Environment, Durham, NH 03824
[4]Canadian Food Inspection Agency, Ottawa, ON K1A0Y9

ABSTRACT

Uncertainty has been widely recognized as one of the most critical issues in predicting the expansion of ecological invasions. The uncertainty associated with the introduction and spread of invasive organisms influences how pest management decisionmakers respond to expanding incursions. In this study, we introduce a new family of modeling techniques to map risks of ecological invasions that combine two potentially conflicting goals: (1) estimating the likelihood of a new organism being established at a given locale; and (2) quantifying the uncertainty of that prediction. Our methodology focuses on the potential for long-distance, human-assisted spread of invasive organisms.

We demonstrate this new approach by analyzing pathways of human-assisted spread (i.e., with commercially transported goods) of the emerald ash borer (*Agrilus planipennis* Fairmaire), a major pest of ash trees in North America. We used a spatial pathway-based model to generate distributions of plausible invasion outcomes over a target geographic region (i.e., eastern North America). We then applied a portfolio-based allocation technique that uses partial stochastic ordering and second-degree stochastic dominance criteria to prioritize the locations where the introduction of the pest with the transport of pest-associated cargoes is most likely.

Our results show that the projected potential of the pest to establish at remote locations is significantly shaped by the amount of epistemic uncertainty in the original model-based forecasts. The estimates based on the portfolio-based allocation better identify major "crossroads" through which the movement of the emerald ash borer with commercial transport is most likely to occur. The system of major expressways in Ontario and Quebec was confirmed as the primary gateway for the pest's expansion throughout the Canadian landscape. Overall, the new approach generates more realistic depiction of long-distance introductions than models that do not account for severe uncertainties, and thus can help design more effective surveillance programs and regulatory responses. The modeling technique is generic and can be applied to assess risks of other invasive organisms when the level of epistemic uncertainty is high.

REVERSE PATHWAY ANALYSIS:
A NEW TOOL FOR RAPID ASSESSMENT OF PEST INVASION RISK

Denys Yemshanov[1], Frank H. Koch[2], Mark Ducey[3] Marty Siltanen[1], and Klaus Koehler[4]

[1]Canadian Forest Service, Great Lakes Forestry Centre, Sault Ste. Marie, ON, P6A2E5
[2]U.S. Forest Service, Southern Research Station, Research Triangle Park, NC 27709
[3]University of New Hampshire, Natural Resources and the Environment, Durham, NH 03824
[4]Canadian Food Inspection Agency, 59 Ottawa, ON K1A0Y9

ABSTRACT

Long-distance introductions of new invasive species are often driven by socioeconomic factors such that traditional "biological" invasion models may not be capable of estimating spread fully and reliably. In this study, we present a new methodology to uncover primary human-mediated vectors and origins of new pest establishments that may be caused by trade, transportation, and/or other economic activities. A reverse pathway analysis answers the question "Where did the species come from before it arrived at the location of interest?" and shows the suspected infestation sources for the location, such as previously infested sites, urban areas, campgrounds or ports of entry.

The analysis is undertaken in three steps. First, we use existing data sources on movement of pest-associated commodities and other economic activities to build a probabilistic pathway model. The model is formulated as a Markovian pathway matrix and allows for quantitative characterization of likelihoods and vectors of new pest introductions from already or likely-to-be infested locations. We then run the pathway model to generate multiple sets of probabilistic predictions of establishment vectors from every potential point of introduction in the transportation network (one point at a time). At the last step, pathway simulations from individual locations of origin are aggregated to a database application that summarizes the locations and likelihoods of the potential origins of an infestation in a given target location of interest. Because the analysis evaluates every possible location as a potential infestation source, the data can be aggregated into a dynamic web application to help communicate the results of the reverse pathway analysis to pest risk professionals and provide real-time decision support for rapid assessments of the potential vectors of human-assisted introductions of invasive pests in North America.

ATTENDEES

23RD USDA INTERAGENCY RESEARCH FORUM ON INVASIVE SPECIES

January 10-13, 2012
Annapolis, Maryland

Kristopher Abell
University of Massachusetts
270 Stockbridge Road
Amherst, MA 01003
kabell@psis.umass.edu

Hathal Al Dhafer
King Saud University
College of Food and Agrculture
Sciences
Riyadh, 11451
hdhafer@ksu.edu.sa

Gillian Allard
FAO of United Nations
Viale delle terme di Caracalla
Rome, 153, Italy
gillian.allard@fao.org

Joan Allen
12050 Government Center Pkwy
Suite 518
Fairfax, VA 22035
joan.allen@fairfaxcounty.gov

Jeremy Allison
404 Life Sciences Building
Louisiana State University
Baton Rouge, LA 70803
jallison@agcenter.lsu.edu

Shu Ambe
PA Department of Agriculture
Bureau of Plant Industry
Harrisburg, PA 17110
sambe@pa.gov

Judy Antipin
U.S. Forest Service
NA State and Private Forestry
Newtown Square, PA 19073
jantipin@fs.fed.us

Ellen Aparicio
501 South Chapel St.
Newark, DE 19713
ellen.aparicio@ars.usda.gov

Arielle Arsenault
University of Vermont
RSENR
Burlington, VT 05405
aarsenault@uvm.edu

Christopher Asaro
Virginia Department of Forestry
900 Natural Resources Dr.
Charlottesville, VA 22903
chris.asaro@dof.virginia.gov

Brittany Barnes
417 Morton Ave
Athens, GA 30605
brittanybarnes8@gmail.com

Roger Barnes
Maryland Dept. Agriculture
50 Harry S. Truman Pkwy.
Annapolis, MD 21401
contractorrogerbarnes@gmail.com

Dick Bean
Maryland Dept. Agriculture
50 Harry S. Truman Pkwy.
Annapolis, MD 21401
beanra@mda.state.md.us

John Bedford
70 Grove Street
Coopersville, MI 49404
bedfordj@michigan.gov

Steve Bell
Maryland Dept. Agriculture
50 Harry S. Truman Pkwy.
Annapolis, MD 21401
contractorstevebell@gmail.com

Robert Bennett
USDA ARS, PSI, IIBBL
10300 Baltimore Ave.
Beltsville, MD 20705
robert.bennett@ars.usda.gov

Ingrid Berlanger
4700 River Road Unit 133
Riverdale, MD 20737
juanita.w.kennedy@aphis.usda.gov

Michael Blackburn
USDA ARS
10300 Baltimore Avenue
Beltsville, MD 20705
mike.blackburn@ars.usda.gov

Ken Bloem
USDA APHIS
1730 Varsity Dr., Suite 400
Raleigh, NC 27606
kenneth.bloem@aphis.usda.gov

George (Jeff) Boettner
132 Bridge St.
Shelburne Falls, MA 01370
boettner@psis.umass.edu

Michael Bohne
U.S. Forest Service
271 Mast Rd.
Durham, NH 03824
mbohne@fs.fed.us

Joyce Bolton
USDA ARS, National Agric. Library
10301 Baltimore Avenue
Beltsville, MD 20705
joyce.bolton@ars.usda.gov

Pierluigi Bonello
Dept. of Plant Pathology
The Ohio State University
Columbus, Ohio 43210
bonello.2@osu.edu

John Borden
Contech Enterprises Inc.
7572 Progress Way
Delta, BC V4G 1E9
john.borden@contech-inc.com

Alicia Bray
Tennessee State University
Agricultural Sciences
McMinnville, TN 37110
abray@tnstate.edu

Kerry Britton
U.S. Forest Service
1601 North Kent Street
Rosslyn Plaza C 4th Floor
Arlington, VA 22209
kbritton01@fs.fed.us

Michael Brown
USDA APHIS PPQ
1715 Southridge Dr.
Jefferson City, MO 65109
michael.e.brown@aphis.usda.gov

Kayla Brownell
155 E. E Paces. Dr.
Athens, GA 30605
brownellk@warnell.uga.edu

Mark Buccowich
US Forest Service
11 Campus Boulevard, Suite 200
Newtown Square, PA 19073
mbuccowich@fs.fed.us

Russ Bulluck
USDA APHIS
1730 Varsity Drive
Raleigh, NC 27606
russ.bulluck@aphis.usda.gov

Barbara Burns
VT Dept. Forests, Parks &
Recreation
35 Fairground Road
Springfield, VT 05156
barbara.burns@state.vt.us

Isis Caetano
521 West Dryden Rd
Freeville, NY 13068
isiscaetano@hotmail.com

Faith Campbell
The Nature Conservancy
4245 North Fairfax Drive
Arlington, VA 22203
fcampbell@tnc.org

Richard Casagrande
University of Rhode Island
Department of Plant Sciences and
Entomology
Kingston, RI 02881
casa@uri.edu

Paul Chaloux
USDA APHIS
4700 River Road
Riverdale, MD 20737
paul.chaloux@aphis.usda.gov

M. Lourdes Chamorro
Systematic Entomology Laboratory
Smithsonian Institution /NMNH,
MRC-168
Washington, D.C. 20013-7012
felicia.bartoszyk@ars.usda.gov

Gary Chastagner
Washington State University
2606 West Pioneer
Puyallup, WA 98371-4900
chastag@wsu.edu

Brian Clark
University of Maryland Extension
6707 Groveton Drive
Clinton, MD 20735
bpclark@umd.edu

Edward Clark
USDA ARS, BARC PSI/IIBB Lab
10300 Baltimore Avenue
Beltsville, MD 20705
edward.clark@ars.usda.gov

David Clement
Univ of MD/HGIC
12005 Homewood Rd
Ellicott City, MD 21042
clement@umd.edu

Sharon Coons
192 North Valley Rd
Harrisonville, PA 17228
scoons@pa.gov

Carla Coots
297 Mays Valley Road
Harriman, TN 37748
cdillin1@utk.edu

Scott Costa
202 Jeffords Hall UVM-PSS
63 Carrigan Dr.
Burlington, VT 5405
scosta@uvm.edu

Ligia Cota Vieira
311 Price Hall
Virginia Tech
Blacksburg, VA 24061
lvieira@vt.edu

Robert Coulson
Entomology-KEL
Texas A&M University
College Station, TX 77843-2475
r-coulson@tamu.edu

Stephen Covell
U.S. Forest Service
Rosslyn Plaza, Building C
Arlington, VA 22209
scovell@fs.fed.us

David Coyle
Warnell School of Forestry and
Natural Resources
University of Georgia
Athens, GA 30602
dcoyle@warnell.uga.edu

Damon Crook
USDA APHIS, PPQ, CPHST
1398 W. Truck Rd.
Buzzards Bay, MA 02542
damon.j.crook@aphis.usda.gov

Mark Dalusky
University of Georgia
Foreset Entomology
Athens, GA 30602
mjdalusk@uga.edu

Vincent D'Amico
Univ. Delaware, Townsend Hall
531 South College Ave.
Newark, DE 19716
vincedamico@gmail.com

Stephanie Darnell
Bayer CropScience
2 T.W. Alexander Drive
Durham, NC 27709
stephanie.darnell@bayer.com

Norman Dart
Virginia Dept. of Agriculture &
Consumer Svcs.
Pathology Lab #229
Richmond, VA 23219
norman.dart@vdacs.virginia.gov

Gina Davis
250 Natural Resources Rd.
115 Ag-Engineering Bldg.
Amsherst, MA 01003
gadavis@psis.umass.edu

Thomas Denholm
USDA APHIS
350 Corporate Boulevard
Trenton, NJ 08691
tom.denholm@aphis.usda.gov

Jenni DeSio
New Jersey Dept. Agriculture
Trenton, NJ 08691
jennifer.desio@ag.state.nj.us

Christine Dieckhoff
USDA ARS
501 South Chapel Street
Newark, DE 19713
christine.dieckhoff@ars.usda.gov

Mary Dix
U.S. Forest Service
1601 North Kent Street
Rosslyn Plaza C 4th Floor
Arlington, VA 22209
mdix@fs.fed.us

Nate Dodds
Mauget
5435 Peck Rd.
Arcadia, CA 91006
mary@mauget.com

Michael Domingue
119 Chemical Ecology Lab
Pennsylvania State University
University Park, PA 16802
mjd29@psu.edu

Leo Donovall
PA Department of Agriculture
Bureau of Plant Industry
Harrisburg, PA 17110
ldonovall@pa.gov

Marla Downing
U.S. Forest Service, FHTET
2150 Centre Ave Build A
Fort Collins, CO 80526
mdowning@fs.fed.us

Tessa M. Dowling
University of Massachusetts
Amherst, MA 01003
temadowling@comcast.net

Jian Duan
USDA ARS, BIIR
501 S. Chapel St.
Newark, DE 19713
jian.duan@ars.usda.gov

Donald Eggen
PA DCNR Bureau of Forestry
208 Airport Drive
Middletown, PA 17057-5027
deggen@pa.gov

Joe Elkinton
University of Massachusetts
Fernald Hall
Amherst, MA 01003
elkington@ent.umass.edu

Monica Errico
USDA APHIS
ALB Detector Dog Program
Newnan, GA 30263
monica.errico@aphis.usda.gov

Eric Ewing
1900 Kanawha Blvd. East
Plant Industries Division
Charleston, WV 25312
eewing@wvda.us

Robert Farrar
USDA ARS IIBBL
10300 Baltimore Ave.
Beltsville, MD 20705
robert.farrar@ars.usda.gov

Mark Faulkenberry
103 Doreen Drive
Hummelstown, PA 17036
markfaulke@yahoo.com

Melissa Fischer
Virginia Tech
216A Price Hall, MC-0319
Blacksburg, VA 24061
mjf43@vt.edu

Christopher Foelker
1 Forestry Dr; 106 Illick Hall
Syracuse, NY 13210
cjfoelke@syr.edu

Joe Francese
USDA APHIS, PPQ, CPHST
1398 W Truck Rd.
Buzzards Bay, MA 02542
joseph.a.francese@aphis.usda.gov

Michelle Frank
U.S. Forest Service
11 Campus Boulevard, Suite 200
Newtown Square, PA 19073
mfrank@fs.fed.us

Roger Fuester
USDA ARS, BIIR
501 S. Chapel St.
Newark, DE 19713
roger.fuester@ars.usda.gov

Kamal Gandhi
University of Georgia
Warnell School
Athens, GA 30605
kgandhi@warnell.uga.edu

Matthew Ginzel
Purdue University
901 W. State Street
West Lafayette, IN 47906
mginzel@purdue.edu

Sara Gomez
89 Albion st
Apt 3
Medford, MD 02155
sara.gomez@tufts.edu

Liahna Gonda-King
11620 Grove Dr
Mukilteo, WA 98275
lgonda-king@my.uri.edu

Ken Gooch
51 Military Road
Amherst, MA 01002
ken.gooch@state.ma.us

Kurt Gottschalk
U.S. Forest Service, NRS
180 Canfield St.
Morgantown, WV 26505
kgottschalk@fs.fed.us

Elizabeth Graham
818 Riley St.
Lansing, MI 48910
egraham3@gmail.com

Jerome Grant
Dept. of Entomol. & Plant
Pathology
2431 Joe Johnson Drive
Knoxville, TN 37996
jgrant@utk.edu

Matt Greenstone
10300 BARC-West
Bldg 011A Rm 214
Beltsville, MD 20705
matt.greenstone@ars.usda.gov

Steve Grossi
Maryland Dept. Agriculture
50 Harry S. Truman Pkwy.
Annapolis, MD 21401

Dawn Gundersen-Rindal
USDA ARS
10300 Baltimore Ave.
Bld 011A Rm 214
Beltsville, MD 20705
dawn.gundersen-rindal@ars.usda.gov

Rodger Gwiazdowski
131 Bridge Street
Amherst, MA 01002
rodger@psis.umass.edu

Robert Haack
U.S. Forest Service, NRS
1407 S. Harrison Rd.
East Lansing, MI 48823
rhaack@fs.fed.us

Rachel Habig
14879 Dumfries Rd
Manassas, VA 20112
rhabig@pwcgov.org

Kevin Hackett
USDA ARS
5601 Sunnyside Avenue
Beltsville, MD 20705
kevin.hackett@ars.usda.gov

Fred Hain
North Carolina State University
P.O. Box 7626
Raleigh, NC 27695
fred_hain@ncsu.edu

Ann Hajek
Department of Entomology
Cornell University
Ithaca, NY 14853-2601
aeh4@cornell.edu

Ryan Hanavan
U.S. Forest Service
271 Mast Rd.
Durham, NH 03824
rhanavan02@fs.fed.us

Larry Hanks
Dept. of Entomology
University of Illinois at Urbana-
Champaign
Urbana, IL 61801
hanks@life.illinois.edu

Jim Hanula
U.S. Forest Service
320 Green St.
Athens, GA 30602-2044
jhanula@fs.fed.us

Robert Harrison
USDA ARS
10300 Baltimore Avenue
Beltsville, MD 20705
robert.l.harrison@ars.usda.gov

Jessica Hartshorn
Univ of Arkansas
Dept of Entomology, AGRI 319
Fayetteville, AR 72701
jhartsho@uark.edu

Stephen Hauss
Delaware Department of Agriculture
2320 South Dupont Hwy
Dover, DE 19943
stephen.hauss@state.de.us

Nathan Havill
U.S. Forest Service, NRS
51 Mill Pond Rd.
Hamden, CT 06514
nphavill@fs.fed.us

Robert Heyd
Michigan Dept. Natural Resources
1990 US 41 South
Marquette, MI 49855
heydr@michigan.gov

Shelley Hicks
Maryland Dept. Agriculture
50 Harry S. Truman Pkwy.
Annapolis, MD 21401
hickssd@mda.state.md.us

Kim Hoelmer
USDA ARS
501 South Chapel St.
Newark, DE 19713
kheolmer@ars.usda.gov

Michael Hoffmann
Cornell University
241 Roberts Hall
Ithaca, NY 14853
mph3@cornell.edu

Anne Hoover
U.S. Forest Service
Rosslyn Plaza, Building C
Arlington, VA 22209
ahoover@fs.fed.us

Kelli Hoover
Pennsylvania State University
501 ASI Building
University Park, PA 16802
kxh25@psu.edu

Judy Hough-Goldstein
University of Delaware
Newark, DE 19713
jhough@udel.edu

Jing Hu
USDA ARS
10300 Baltimore Ave. BARC-West
Beltsville, MD 20705
jing.hu@ars.usda.gov

Leland Humble
Natural Resources Canada
506 West Burnside Rd.
Victoria, BC V8Z 1M5
leland.humble@nrcan.gc.ca

Lisa Jackson
USDA APHIS
1730 Varsity Dr., Ste. 400
Raleigh, NC 27615
lisa.d.jackson@aphis.usda.gov

Michael Jacobson
Pennsylvania State University
501 ASI Bldg.
University Park, PA 16802
mgj2@psu.edu

Nina Jenkins
107 Merkle Laboratory
University Park
State College, PA 16802
nej2@psu.edu

David Jennings
14329 Wedgewood Circle #201
Tampa, FL 33613
david.e.jennings@gmail.com

Amy Johnson
USDA ARS
501 South Chapel St.
Newark, DE 19713
amjohns@udel.edu

Anne Jones
Entomology Dept.
VA Tech
Blacksburg, VA 24061
annej@vt.edu

Cera Jones
82 College Circle
Dahlonega, Georgia 30597
cejones@northgeorgia.edu

Matt Kasson
Pennsylvania State University
401 Buckhart Lab.
University Park, PA 16802
mtk178@psu.edu

Melody Keena
U.S. Forest Service, NRS
51 Mill Pond Rd.
Hamden, CT 06514
mkeena@fs.fed.us

Marc Kenis
CABI Europe-Switzerland
Delemont, 2800, Switzerland
m.kenis@cabi.org

Ryan Kepler
Cornell University
126 Garden Ave.
Ithaca, NY 14853
rmkepler@gmail.com

Kathleen Kidd
NCDA&CS, Plant Industry
Division
1060 Mail Service Center
Raleigh, NC 27699
kathleen.kidd@ncagr.gov

Troy Kimoto
Suite 400
4321 Still Creek Drive
Burnaby, BC V5C 6S7
troy.kimoto@inspection.gc.ca

Kier Klepzig
U.S. Forest Service
200 WT Weaver Blvd.
Asheville, NC 28804
kklepzig@fs.fed.us

MaryJo Klovensky
Maryland Dept. Agriculture
50 Harry S. Truman Pkwy.
Annapolis, MD 21401
crouchdl@mda.state.md.us

Frank Koch
3041 Cornwallis Rd
P.O. Box 12254
Research Triangle Park, NC 27709
fhkoch@fs.fed.us

Klaus Koehler
59 Camelot Drive
Ottawa, K1A 0Y9
klaus.koehler@inspection.gc.ca

Ryotaro Komura
Ishikawa National College of
Technology
Kitacyujo, Tsubata
Ishikawa, 929-0392
komura@gm.ishikawa-nct.ac.jp

Kay Kromm
Nebraska Dept. Agriculture
301 Centennial Mall South
Lincoln, NE 68509
kay.kromm@nebraska.gov

Jimmy Kroon
Delaware Department of Agriculture
2320 South Dupont Hwy
Dover, DE 19943
jimmy.kroon@state.de.us

Faith Kuehn
Delaware Department of Agriculture
2320 South Dupont Highway
Dover, DE 19901
faith.kuehn@state.de.us

Daniel Kuhar
USDA ARS
10300 Baltimore Ave
Beltsville, MD 20705
daniel.kuhar@ars.usda.gov

Craig Kuhn
Maryland Dept. Agriculture
P.O. Box 502
Forest Hill, MD 21050
northeastfpm@gmail.com

Ken Kukorowski
Bayer Environmental Science
2 Alexander Drive
Research Triangle Park, NC 27709
ken.kukorowski@bayer.com

Paul Kurtz
P.O. Box 330
Trenton, NJ 08625
pjkurtz@hotmail.com

Kerrie Kyde
MD DNR-WHS
11960 Clopper Road
Gaithersburg, MD 20878
kkyde@dnr.state.md.us

James LaBonte
Oregon Dept. Agriculture
635 Capitol St., NE
Salem, OR 97301
jlabonte@oda.state.or.us

Ashley Lamb
University of Tennessee
2431 Joe Johnson Dr.
Knoxville, TN 37996
alamb6@utk.edu

Douglas LeDoux
Missouri Department of Agriculture
P.O. Box 630
Jefferson City, MO 65102
douglas.ledoux@mda.mo.gov

Jonathan Lelito
5936 Ford Court
Suite 200
Brighton, MI 48116
jonathan.lelito@aphis.usda.gov

Mike Leventry
P.O. Box 501
Kennett Square, PA 19348
mleventry@longwoodgardens.org

Phil Lewis
USDA, APHIS, PPQ, CPHST
1398 W. Truck Road
Buzzards Bay, MA 02542
phillip.a.lewis@aphis.usda.gov

John Libs
Phyllom BioProducts
922 SanLeandro Ave., Ste. F
Mountain View, CA 94031
johnlibs@phyllom.com

Andrew Liebhold
U.S. Forest Service, NRS
180 Canfield St.
Morgantown, WV 26505
aliebhold@fs.fed.us

Harri Liljalehto
632 Homewood Avenue
Peterborough, ON K9J 4V5
hliljalehto@gmail.com

Steven Lingafelter
Systematic Entomology Laboratory
Smithsonian Institution - NMNH
Washington, DC 20013-7012
steven.lingafelter@ars.usda.gov

Houping Liu
Pennsylvania DCNR
Middletown, PA 17057
brian.cm.liu@gmail.com

Elizabeth Long
University of Tennessee
2431 Joe Johnson Drive, 205 PSB
Knoxville, TN 37996-4560
ealong@utk.edu

Douglas Luster
USDA ARS FDWSRU
1301 Ditto Ave.
Ft. Detrick, MD 21702
doug.luster@ars.usda.gov

John Lydon
USDA ARS
5601 Sunnyside Avenue
Beltsville, MD 20705
john.lydon@ars.usda.gov

Christopher Maier
CT Agricultural Experiment Station
P.O. Box 1106
New Haven, CT 06504-1106
chris.maier@ct.gov

Steve Malan
Maryland Dept. Agriculture
50 Harry S. Truman Pkwy.
Annapolis, MD 21401
malansc@mda.state.md.us

Mary Kay Malinoski
12005 Homewood Rd
University of Maryland/HGIC
Ellicott City, MD 21042
mkmal@umd.edu

Gary Man
U.S. Forest Service
Rosslyn Plaza, Building C
Arlington, VA 22209
gman@fs.fed.us

Christine Markham
USDA APHIS
1730 Varsity Dr.
Raleigh, NC 27616
christine.markham@aphis.usda.gov

Beth McClelland
VA Dept. Agric. & Consumer
Affairs
234 W. Shirley Avenue
Warrenton, VA 20186
beth.mcclelland@vdacs.virginia.gov

Elizabeth McKenzie
University of Massachusetts
Fernald Hall
Amherst, MA 01003
emckenzie@student.umass.edu

Tim McNary
USDA APHIS
2150 Centre Ave., Bldg. B3E10
Fort Collins, CO 80526
timothy.j.mcnary@usda.gov

Ace Lynn-Miller
University of Arkansas
Dept of Entomology, AGRI 319
Fayetteville, AR 72701
alynnmil@uark.eduJorge

Vitaly Minchenko
Science & Technology Group
Russian Embassy
2650 Wisconsin Ave., NW
Washington, DC
vitaly_mink@yahoo.com

Jim Marra
3939 Cleveland Ave.
Olympia, WA 98501
jmarra@agr.wa.gov

Debra Martin
12475 Newfound Falls Lane
Doswell, VA 23047
debra.martin@vdacs.virginia.gov

Phyllis Martin
USDA/ARS/IIBBL
10300 Baltimore Ave.
Beltsville, MD 20705
phyllis.martin@ars.usda.gov

Vic Mastro
USDA APHIS, PPQ
1398 West Truck Road
Buzzards Bay, MA 02542
vic.mastro@aphis.usda.gov

David Mausel
Menominee Tribal Enterprises-
Forestry Center
P.O. Box 10
Neopit, WI 54150
davidm@mtewood.com

Mark Mayer
NJ Dept. of Agriculture
Phillip Alampi Beneficial Insect Lab
Trenton, NJ 08625
mark.mayer@ag.state.nj.us

Albert Mayfield
200 W.T. Weaver Blvd.
Asheville, NC 28804
amayfield02@fs.fed.us

Tom McAvoy
Dept. of Entomology
Virginia Tech
Blacksburg, VA 24061
tmcavoy@vt.edu

Richard McDonald
194 Shull's Hollar
Sugar Grove, NC 28679
drmcbug@skybest.com

Michael McManus
U.S.Forest Service, Retired
51 Mill Pond Rd.
Hamden, CT 06514
mlmcmanus@fs.fed.us

Angela Mech
417 Morton Ave
Athens, GA 30605
angmech@gmail.com

Peter Meng
Pennsylvania State University
510 Ag and Life Sciences Bldg.
University Park, PA 16801
meng.peter@psu.edu

Manfred Mielke
U.S. Forest Service
11 Campus Boulevard, Suite 200
Newtown Square, PA 19073
mmielke@fs.fed.us

Jocelyn Millar
Dept of Entomology
University of California, Riverside
Riverside, CA 92521
jocelyn.millar@ucr.edu

Dan Miller
U.S. Forest Service
320 Green Street
Athens, GA 30602
dmiller03@fs.fed.us

Wayne Millington
424 Forest Resources Building
University Park, PA 16802
wayne_millington@nps.gov

Bruce Moltzan
U.S. Forest Service
Rosslyn Plaza, Building C
Arlington, VA 22209
bmoltzan@fs.fed.us

Melanie Newfield
Ministry of Agriculture and Forestry
P.O. Box 2526
Wellington, 6140, New Zealand
melanie.newfield@maf.govt.nz

Stephen Nicholson
Valent BioSciences
2704 Orser Rd.
Elginburg, ON K0H 1M6
stephen.nicholson@valent.com

Robert Nowierski
800 Ninth Street SW
Washington, DC 20024
rnowierski@nfia.usda.gov

Brad Onken
U.S. Forest Service
180 Canfield Street
Morgantown, WV 26505
bonken@fs.fed.us

Emmanuel Opumni-Frimpong
Forestry Research Inst.-Ghana
P.O. Box 63
Kumasi, Ghana
eopunifr@mtu.edu

Andrei Orlinski
EPPO
21 Boulevard Richard Lenoir
Paris, France 75011
orlinski@eppo.fr

Mary Orr
1124 Finch Avenue West, Unit #2
Toronto, L7B 1K4
mary.orr@inspection.gc.ca

Kelly Oten
948 Shining Wire Way
Morrisville, NC 27560
klfelder@ncsu.edu

Cristi Palmer
Rutgers University
IR-4
New Brunswick, NJ, 08540
palmer@aesop.rutgers.edu

Patrick Parkman
Entomology & Plant Pathology
Dept.
2431 Joe Johnson Dr., 205 PSB
Knoxville, TN 37996-4560
jparkman@utk.edu

Gregory Parra
USDA APHIS
1730 Varsity Drive
Raleigh, NC 27606
greg.r.parra@aphis.usda.gov

Dylan Parry
State Univeristy of New York
Enviornmental Science & Forestry
Syracuse, NY 13210
dparry@esf.edu

Joshua Pezet
University of Massachusetts
250 Natural Resources Rd.
Amherst, MA 01003
jpezet@cns.umass.edu

Scott Pfister
USDA APHIS
4700 River Road
Riverdale, MD 20737
scott.e.pfister@aphis.usda.gov

Charles Pickett
Maryland Dept. Agriculture
50 Harry S, Truman Pkwy.
Annapolis, MD 21401
contractorcharlespickett@gmail.com

John Podgwaite
U.S. Forest Service, NRS
51 Mill Pond Rd.
Hamden, CT 06514
jpodgwaite@fs.fed.us

Therese Poland
U.S. Forest Service
1407 S. Harrison Road
East Lansing, MI 48823
tpoland@fs.fed.us

Steve Powell
Ellington Agricultural Center
Division of Regulatory Services
Nashville, TN 37204
steve.powell@tn.gov

Evan Preisser
University of Rhode Island
Dept. Plant Pathology-Entomology
Kingston, RI 02881
preisser@uri.edu

Timothy Price
4455 Big Spring Rd
Blain, PA 17006
tiprice@pa.gov

Martin Proctor
Maryland Dept. Agriculture
50 Harry S. Truman Pkwy.
Annapolis, MD 21401
contractormartinproctor@gmail.com

Bob Rabaglia
U.S. Forest Service
Rosslyn Plaza, Building C
Arlington, VA 22209
brabaglia@fs.fed.us

Laura Radville
161 Federal Way
Apt 304
Johnston, RI 02919
laura.radville@gmail.com

Jamie Rafter
P.O. Box 1435
Kingston, RI 2881
jamierafter@gmail.com

Brendon Reardon
USDA APHIS
4700 River Rd.
Riverdale, MD 20737
brendon.reardon@aphis.usda.gov

Richard Reardon
U.S. Forest Service
180 Canfield Street
Morgantown, WV 26505
rreardon@fs.fed.us

Karen Rane
University of Maryland
4112 Plant Sciences
College Park, MD 20742
rane@umd.edu

Christine Rega
1200 W Creek Village Dr., Apt G4
Elkton, MD 21921
christinerega@gmail.com

Rusty Rhea
200 WT Weaver Blvd
Asheville, NC 28804
rrhea@fs.fed.us

Stefan Richard
921 College Hill Rd.
Fredericton, NB E3C1V1
srichard@sylvar.ca

Dana Rhodes
PA Department of Agriculture
Bureau of Plant Industry
Harrisburg, PA 17110
danrhodes@pa.gov

Kimberly Rice
50 Harry S. Truman Pkwy.
Annapolis, MD 21401
halletdc@mda.state.md.us

John Riggins
121 Edgewood Drive
Starkville, MS 39759
johnjriggins@gmail.com

Jim Rollins
Mauget
5435 Peck Rd.
Arcadia, CA 91006
jim@mauget.com

Scott Salom
216 Price Hall Mail Code 0319
Department of Entomology
Blacksburg, VA 24061
salom@vt.edu

Macias-Samano
7061 Merritt Ave.
Burnaby, BC V5J 4R7
jorge@semiochemical.com

Frank Sapio
U.S., Forest Service, FHTET
2150 Centre Ave, Bld A
Fort Collins, CO 80525
fsapio@fs.fed.us

Chris Sargent
University of Maryland
4112 Plant Sciences Bldg.
College Park, MD 20742
csargen1@umd.edu

Linda Saunders
USDA ARS
501 South Chapel St.
Newark, DE 19713
linda.saunders@ars.usda.gov

Taylor Scarr
Ontario Ministry of Natural
Resources
70 Foster Drive
Sault Ste. Marie, ON P6A 6V5
taylor.scarr@ontario.ca

Noel Schneeberger
U.S. Forest Service
11 Campus Boulevard, Suite 200
Newtown Square, PA 19073
nschneeberger@fs.fed.us

Kurt Schwartau
Phyllom, LLC
39335 Granite Bay Pl.
Davis, CA 95616
kurtschwartau@phyllom.com

Jean Scott
Rainbow Tree Care
P.O. Box 5241
Salisbury, MD 21802
jscott@treecarescience.com

Steven Seybold
University of California
Davis, CA 95616
sseybold@fs.fed.us

Michael Simmons
45 1/2 Market Street
Newburyport, MA 01950
mjx28@unh.edu

Michael Smith
501 South Chapel St.
Newark, DE 19713
michael.smith@ars.usda.gov

John Snitzer
P.O. Box 39
Dickerson, MD 20842
navajuela@comcast.net

Amy Snyder
Department of Entomology
709 Harding Rd
Blacksburg, VA 24060
amys6@vt.edu

Robert Spaide
University of Tennessee
2431 Joe Johnson Drive, 205 PSB
Knoxville, TN 37996-4560
rspaide@utk.edu

Michael Sparks
10300 Baltimore Ave
Bld 011A Rm 214
Beltsville, MD 20707
michael.sparks@ars.usda.gov

Julie Spaulding
USDA APHIS
4700 River Rd.
Riverdale, MD 20737
julie.s.spaulding@aphis.usda.gov

Michael Stefan
USDA APHIS, PPQ, CPHST
1730 Varsity Dr
Raleigh, NC 27606
michael.b.stefan@aphis.usda.gov

Fred Stephen
Department of Entomology
University of Arkansas
Fayetteville, AK 72701
fstephen@uark.edu

Sam Stokes
50 Harry S. Truman Pkwy.
Annapolis, MD 21401
contractorsamstokes@gmail.com

Douglas Streett
2500 Shreveport Highway
Pineville, LA 71303
dastreett@fs.fed.us

Elizabeth Sussky
Natural Resources Conservation
University of Massachusetts
Amherst, MA 01003
esussky@student.umass.edu

Jil Swearingen
National Park Service
4598 MacArthur Blvd. NW
Washington, DC 20007
jil_swearingen@nps.gov

Jon Sweeney
NRCan-Canadian Forest Service
1350 Regent Street
Fredericton, NB E3B5P7
jsweeney@nrcan.gc.ca

Bob Tatman
Maryland Dept. Agriculture
50 Harry S. Truman Pkwy.
Annapolis, MD 21401
tatman.bob@gmail.com

Daria Tatman
USDA ARS
501 South Chapel St.
Newark, DE 19713
daria.tatman@ars.usda.gov

Mark Taylor
27722 Nanticoke Road, Unit 2
Salisbury, MD 21801
taylormc@mda.state.md.us

Philip Taylor
USDA ARS, BIIR
501 S. Chapel St.
Newark, DE 19713
philip.taylor@ars.usda.gov

Steven Teale
State Univeristy of New York
Enviornmental Science & Forestry
Syracuse, NY 13210
sateale@esf.edu

Elizabeth Tewksbury
University of Rhode Island
210C Woodward Hall
Kingston, RI 02881
lisat@uri.edu

Biff Thompson
51 Main St
Lonaconing, MD 21539
bifft7@verizon.net

Brian Thompson
University of Maryland
4112 Plant Science Bldg.
College Park, MD 20742
bthomps7@umd.edu

Robert Tichenor
USDA APHIS, PPQ
4700 River Rd Unit 133
Riverdale, MD 20737
robert.h.tichenor@aphis.usda.gov

Tim Tomon
1900 Kanawha Blvd. East
Plant Industries Division
Charleston, WV 25305
ttomon@wvda.us

Matthew Travis
USDA APHIS, PPQ
2200 Broening Hwy
Baltimore, MD 21224
matthew.a.travis@aphis.usda.gov

Robert Trickel
North Carolina Forest Service
1616 Mail Service Center
Raleigh, NC 27539-1616
rob.trickel@ncagr.gov

Talbot Trotter
U.S. Forest Service
51 Mill Pond Rd.
Hamden, CT 06514
rttrotter@fs.fed.us

Robert Trumbule
10300 Baltimore Avenue
Bldg. 308, Rm. 305, BARC-E
Beltsville, MD 20705
rtrumbule@erols.com

Todd Ugine
Cornell University
Ithaca, NY 14853
tau2@cornell.edu

Roy Van Driesche
PSIS/Entomology
University of Massachusetts
Amherst, MA 01003
vandries@cns.umass.edu

John Vandenberg
USDA ARS
Robert W Holley Center for
Agriculture and Health
Ithaca, NY 14853
jdv3@cornell.edu

Joseph Vukovich
USDA APHIS, PPQ
2200 Broening Highway
Baltimore, MD 21224
joseph.m.vukovich@aphis.usda.gov

Kimberly Wallin
U.S. Forest Service, NRS
University of Vermont-RSENR
Burlington, VT 05405
kwallin@uvm.edu

Baode Wang
USDA APHIS, PPQ, CPHST
Buzzards Bay, MA 02542
baode.wang@aphis.usda.gov

Aaron Weed
Ecology & Evolutionary Biology
Dartmouth College
Dartmouth, NH 03755
aaron.s.weed@dartmouth.edu

Ron Weeks
USDA APHIS
901 Main Campus Dr.
Raleigh, NC 27606
rdweeks@aphis.usda.gov

Geoff White
USDA ARS
10300 Baltimore Ave.
Beltsville, MD 20705
geoffrey.white@ars.usda.gov

Mark Whitmore
Cornell University
Dept. of Natural Resources
Ithaca, NY 14853
mcw42@cornell.edu

Richard Wilson
70 Foster Drive
Sault Ste. Marie, ON P6A 3V1
richard.wilson@ontario.ca

Michael Wingfield
University of Pretoria
Forestry & Agricultural
Biotechnology Institute
Pretoria, 0002 South Africa
mike.wingfield@fabi.up.ac.za

Tom Woods
Phyllom, LLC
8307 Linville Oaks Dr.
Oak Ridge, NC 27310
pratita76@gmail.com

Jinquan Wu
501 South Chapel Street
Newark, DE 19713
jinquanw@udel.edu

Denys Yemshanov
Natural Resources Canada
1219 Queen Street East
Sault Ste. Marie, ON P6A 2E5
dyemshan@nrcan.gc.ca

James Young
USDA APHIS, PPQ
2200 Broening Highway
Baltimore, MD 21224
jim.d.young@aphis.usda.gov

Amos Ziegler
Michigan State University
Department of Entomology
East Lansing, MI 48824
ziegler2@msu.edu

McManus, Katherine A; Gottschalk, Kurt W., eds. 2013. **Proceedings. 23rd U.S. Department of Agriculture interagency research forum on invasive species 2012;** 2012 January 10-13; Annapolis, MD. Gen. Tech. Rep. NRS-P-114. Newtown Square, PA: U.S. Department of Agriculture, Forest Service, Northern Research Station. 126 p.

Contains abstracts and papers of 75 oral and poster presentations on invasive species biology, molecular biology, ecology, impacts, and management presented at the annual U.S. Department of Agriculture Interagency Research Forum on Invasive Species.

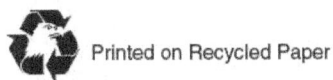 Printed on Recycled Paper

Northern Research Station

www.nrs.fs.fed.us